I0030737

Advanced Business for Social Benefits

Profit from Serving Social Needs Well

Donald Mitchell

Author of *Advanced Business*,
Advanced Business for Innovation,
Business Basics, *Excellent Leadership*,
and *Excellent Solutions*
Coauthor of *The 2,000 Percent Solution* and
The 2,000 Percent Squared Solution

400 Year Project Press
Weston, Massachusetts
United States of America

Other 400 Year Project Books by Donald Mitchell

The 2,000 Percent Solution (with Carol Coles and Robert Metz)

The Portable 2,000 Percent Solution (with Carol Coles)

The 2,000 Percent Solution Workbook (with Carol Coles)

The 2,000 Percent Squared Solution (with Carol Coles)

The Irresistible Growth Enterprise (with Carol Coles)

The Ultimate Competitive Advantage (with Carol Coles)

Adventures of an Optimist

Witnessing Made Easy (with Bishop Dale P. Combs, Lisa Combs, Jim Barbarossa, and Carla Barbarossa)

Ways You Can Witness (with Cherie Hill, Roger de Brabant, Drew Dickens, Gael Torcise, Wendy Lobos, Herpha Jane Obod, and Gisele Umugiraneza)

2,000 Percent Living

Help Wanted

The 2,000 Percent Nation

Business Basics

Excellent Solutions (For-Profit and Nonprofit Editions)

Excellent Leadership

Advanced Business

Advanced Business for Innovation

Advanced Business for Social Benefits

Profit from Serving Social Needs Well

Copyright © 2007, 2011, 2012, 2013, 2015 by Donald W. Mitchell.
All rights reserved.

Image Copyright © 2015 by Derrick Z. Jackson.
All rights reserved.

No part of this publication may be reproduced distributed, or transmitted in any form or by any means, including photocopying, recording, or other electronic or mechanical methods without the prior written permission of the publisher, except in the case of brief quotations embodied in critical reviews and certain other noncommercial uses permitted by copyright law.

Scripture taken from the New King James Version®
Copyright ©1982 by Thomas Nelson, Inc.
Used by permission. All rights reserved.

ISBN: 978-0692453933
0692453938

For information, contact:

Donald W. Mitchell
400 Year Project Press
P.O. Box 302
Weston, Massachusetts 02493
781-647-4211

Published in the United States of America

This book is dedicated to:

Members of The Billionaire Entrepreneurs' Master Mind

May quickly and easily providing vast increases in social benefits that profit their organizations always be ahead of them!

And their spouses, their children and grandchildren, and their descendants

May this book help them to always focus on the Lord and doing His will!

Contents

Acknowledgments ..... *ix*

Foreword ..... *xi*

Introduction ..... *xv*

Lesson One: Benefit Selection 1

Lesson Two: Evaluate Customer Focus 9

Lesson Three: Adjust End-User Focus 15

Lesson Four: Select Suppliers 23

Lesson Five: Energize Employees 29

Lesson Six: Engage Employees' Families 37

Lesson Seven: Open Up Owners 45

Lesson Eight: Add Dream-Team Partners 53

Lesson Nine: Add Different Kinds of Distributors 63

Lesson Ten: Add Volunteers 71

Lesson Eleven: Raise Awareness and Gain Information with the Help of Interested Strangers 79

Lesson Twelve: Co-Opt Competitors 87

Lesson Thirteen: Connect to Communities You Serve 97

Lesson Fourteen: Attract Government Support 107

Lesson Fifteen: Interest and Enlist Experts 117

Lesson Sixteen: Gain Support from Authorities 123

Lesson Seventeen: Gain Support from Foundations........................135
Lesson Eighteen: Attract and Involve the General Public.............143
Lesson Nineteen: Build a Foundation for an Irresistible Cause.....153
Lesson Twenty: Prepare a Path to the Irresistible Cause...............159
Lesson Twenty-One: Polish the Story of Your Irresistible Cause...165
Lesson Twenty-Two: Plan an Unmistakable Launch of Your Irresistible Cause...171
Lesson Twenty-Three: Plan Commitment-Building Experiences for Your Irresistible Cause...................................177
Lesson Twenty-Four: Attract Large Numbers of People to Commitment-Building Experiences..183
Lesson Twenty-Five: Train People to Perform Key Tasks...........189
Lesson Twenty-Six: Create a Foundation for Replacing a Government Activity 193
Lesson Twenty-Seven: Replace a Government Activity by Gaining Financing for Beneficiaries...199
Lesson Twenty-Eight: Replace a Government Activity with Private Financing for Beneficiaries 205
Lesson Twenty-Nine: Replace a Government Activity by Directly Financing Beneficiaries 211
Lesson Thirty: Replace a Government Activity by Showing Beneficiaries How to Finance Themselves.................................217
Lesson Thirty-One: Replace a Private-Enterprise Activity............223
Lesson Thirty-Two: Replace a Private-Enterprise Activity with High Social Costs 229

Lesson Thirty-Three: Replace a Private-Enterprise Activity Providing Few Social Benefits 235

Lesson Thirty-Four: Replace a Private-Enterprise Activity by Greatly Increasing Social Benefits 241

Afterword *247*

Appendix One: Donald Mitchell's Testimony *249*

Appendix Two: Brief Profiles of Organizations from Their Web Sites *257*

Acknowledgments

Oh, give thanks to the LORD!
Call upon His name;
Make known His deeds among the peoples!

– 1 Chronicles 16:8 (NKJV)

I thank Almighty God, our Heavenly Father, for creating the universe and all the people on the Earth; our Lord and Savior, Jesus Christ, for providing the way for us to gain Salvation; and the Holy Spirit for guiding our daily paths towards repentance and righteousness. I also humbly acknowledge the perfect guidance I received from God through the Holy Spirit and His Word to write this book.

I feel deeply honored by Deremiah *CPE (*Customer Passion Evangelist) having written this book's excellent Foreword. I have been blessed to know him from afar for many years. His passion for serving others and compassion for those who need help have been a continuing source of inspiration for me. While praying for Heavenly guidance about who should write the Foreword, the Holy Spirit whispered Deremiah's name. I immediately realized the brilliance of God's direction. Deremiah has long been living this book's subject through Customer Passion Evangelizm* (*Deremiah's way of personalizing what he does), a creative think tank guiding organizations and individuals into the future by getting them back to their first love ... the love of serving and evangelizing customers with passion. In the Foreword, Deremiah shares part of his story to help you better appreciate how this book can help you.

I am grateful to Peter Drucker for encouraging me to write about 2,000 percent solutions (ways of accomplishing 20 times more with the same or less time, effort, and resources) and to seek ever-simpler ways to help people learn to employ them. His faith in this method for solving problems caused me to take much more seriously the opportunity to share what I had been doing.

I appreciate all those who have permitted me to share with them 2,000 percent solution methods and The 400 Year Project's work in improving far beyond them. I thank those who have applied what they learned for all the insights I have gained from observing their wonderful work.

I can never thank my family enough for allowing me the time and peace to work on such a huge and awe-inspiring project for God. They made many sacrifices without complaining and have been a continual inspiration.

I appreciate my many clients who held off on their demands for my help so that this project could receive the attention it required. Their financial support also made it possible for me to give this time to the Lord and to invest in the book's expenses.

Finally, I am most appreciative of the many fine improvements that my editor, Bernice Pettinato, made in the text. This is the eighteenth book where she has helped me to make the messages clearer and more pleasant to read. As always, she was a delight to work with. Her kindness made the writing much easier. I value all she has taught me about writing. I look forward to learning new lessons from her during future books.

I accept sole responsibility for any remaining errors and apologize to my readers for any difficulties and inconvenience that they encounter as a consequence.

Foreword

To say you're about to love every minute you spend reading *Advanced Business for Social Benefits* would most definitely be an understatement. I read it twice before I wrote this Foreword, and that's why I'm honored and humbled to have Dr. Don Mitchell invite me to write the Foreword to what I believe is the foundational landmark book for our new era in conscious capitalism. We are at an interesting fork in the road where the global marketplace is trying to deal with both an advance in our new birthright of technological economic opportunities and the reality of individuals trapped in the archaic myths of a world operating with broken tools from the Industrial Age. At the same time that millionaires are popping up everywhere ... even among our children ... the sweet and innocent children in a lot of countries still live in the bitterness of poverty. So what is to come of the next generation? What will happen with our children's children if we fail or, worse yet, if we just flat out refuse to have a transformation in our thinking for creating greater social benefits — a transformation that allows us to see more clearly the results we could be experiencing right now?

Having spent decades in the trenches providing social benefits, holding children's hands and crying with them during their most challenging moments, I understand the importance of the ideas in this book. I appreciate the tremendous value it will bring long after we are gone, if we read the words and act on the powerful advice we are given. Whether you're an executive, a partner, a manager, a donor, or a volunteer, you now hold in your hands a complete system for how to add new life, new revenues, and new opportunities, and create a social movement that can have impact. If you implement the ideas that will inspire you, direct you, educate you, and cause you to understand the immense value you're currently understating in your organization, you will win. Dr. Don Mitchell has set the table for us to participate in this new social breakthrough — a breakthrough that will exponentially multiply our revenue, profits, finances, value, innovativeness, careers, and spiritual fruitfulness as for-profit enterprises and individuals by serving the most important social needs much more effectively than they are provided for today.

Advanced Business for Social Benefits brings a bright light to three topics of importance if our most effective organizations are to properly provide for the world everyone could and should be living in:

1. Identifying the most useful benefits to provide and increase
2. Developing and adjusting relationships with those our organizations touch so that more can be accomplished
3. Providing 20 times more social benefits while using no more resources than are being applied today

Much of what Dr. Mitchell has shared in the pages of this book awakens my most memorable experiences from my early days working with Verlyn "Swede" Roskam. Swede, as he was so dearly called, was a Christian man who had a dream for a new start-up venture he initiated while working as a vice president of sales for Oil Dri Corporation of America. Without any venture capital, angel investors, or seed money, using a concept he had read about on the subject of bartering, he embarked on an unconventional way of providing scholarships for struggling students in small colleges.

Once a struggling student at Wentworth Military Academy, on the verge of dropping out in his senior year because he didn't have the money to finish college, he received a life-changing donation. He tells a story of how he was blessed by a husband and wife who lost their only son during World War II. They decided to take the insurance money from his policy and invest in a student who was struggling financially. Swede was that student. The donation helped him get through college. He never forgot that and it's what drove him to start EAL, Educational Assistance Limited, in a bedroom in their home with his wife, Martha Roskam. Soon, using only a few of the strategies described here in Dr. Mitchell's book, Swede Roskam was experiencing the 2,000 percent solution as he began to embark on providing social benefits for the good of others. He immediately began receiving so many donations of obsolete inventory from U.S. companies such as Allied Van Lines, Monsanto, Ciba Geigy, Amoco, and Nabisco that he was immediately able to get a few colleges to agree to offer scholarships through the program.

The colleges accepted these donations of obsolete inventory — inventory that still had value which had not been fully depreciated — and they provided write-offs to the corporations in exchange. The inventory included anything from furniture to automobiles and everything in between.

It was at this time that I met Swede and Martha Roskam. I was at North Park University, which was the first college to agree to participate in the program. Similar to Swede, I needed some additional money to finish my last year of college. The scholarship EAL provided put me among the first college students to receive a scholarship through the program.

Because of my personal due diligence and follow-through by keeping in contact with Swede and Martha, I was eventually blessed with an even greater opportunity. Upon graduation I was having trouble finding a job that would allow me to leverage my two degrees in accounting and art. At that same exact time Swede and Martha were looking for someone to hire to take the burden off of them since Swede was already working a full-time job. They finally bit the bullet and decided that hiring me was the best thing to do. Although Swede had no money to pay me, he bartered, again, for my salary by going directly to his boss, Richard M. Jaffee, the CEO of Oil Dri, who felt that the broader impact Swede was having on American small colleges was so important that he never saw it as a conflict of interest. He not only paid my salary but he also made office space available. This arrangement also included telephones, computers, copiers, and other miscellaneous items, all in the luxury of downtown Chicago on Michigan Avenue.

I can assure you that Richard M. Jaffee saw the tremendous social benefits of doing this because he even included our picture and story in his company's annual report. Do you think this social benefit improved his company's image or influenced his revenue? I can assure you that it did. As a result of Oil Dri's corporate partnership with our nonprofit organization, we scaled so much faster. Our unconventional approaches to bartering and partnering made EAL a success. But this partnership was not only across industries, it was also across religions as Swede Roskam, a caring Christian man, partnered with Richard M. Jaffe, a caring Jewish man. It was through this experience that my ideas for Customer Passion Evangelizm (the "z" is no typo ... it's the way I personalize what I do) grew because I saw, first-hand, how serving with passion helped everything we did.

Now you get a chance to peel back the pages of this great book written by Dr. Don Mitchell, and you get to connect the dots to my own story to see how many different social-benefit strategies we actually used. I can assure you that if we would have only had Dr. Mitchell's *Advanced Business for Social Benefits*, we would have gone so much further, so much more easily, and so much faster that we would have eclipsed the results we achieved.

– Deremiah *CPE

Deremiah *CPE is a trusted strategic advisor to founders, CEOs, COOs, and small business owners. He is also one of the Marketingprofs.com Top 25 Marketing Experts and winner of the coveted Lifetime Achievement Award by Nightingale Conant for dedicating his life to serving at-risk children by using Customer Passion Evangelizm.

St. Charles, Illinois, USA
May 2015

Introduction

"You are the light of the world.
A city that is set on a hill cannot be hidden.

"Nor do they light a lamp and
put it under a basket,
but on a lampstand,
and it gives light
to all who are in the house."

— Matthew 5:14-15 (NKJV)

The information in *Advanced Business for Social Benefits: Profit from Serving Social Needs Well* has been selected from among The 400 Year Project's most powerful, easily appreciated, and readily applicable lessons during the project's 20 years of research and practice. Many of these lessons were initially developed during 2012 and 2013 for The Billionaire Entrepreneurs' Master Mind, a consortium of entrepreneurs learning and applying the latest generation of The 400 Year Project's best practices to achieve success beyond the usual kinds of breakthroughs. Versions of seven lessons in *Advanced Business for Social Benefits* also appear in the for-profit edition of *Excellent Solutions* (400 Year Project Press, 2014). All the lessons have deep roots in earlier research and testing done by Outstanding Chief Executive Officers, a partnership of global leaders Carol Coles and I directed to develop many of the current best practices for helpfully profiting from serving social needs. All of the lessons have been updated and improved to increase their usefulness.

Advanced Business for Social Benefits: Profit from Serving Social Needs Well is different from many other business books about serving the public in profitable ways by primarily paying attention to what a company can do to solve major social problems, improve its business model to fit the solutions, and apply the model for serving major public needs in ways to benefit all stakeholders. As such, this book looks deeply at what benefits to provide, who to engage in such provisions, how to increase participation in the work, and how to make the necessary changes. In taking this approach, however, I happily acknowledge that research concerning increasing the effectiveness of social enterprises can be applied in conjunction with the lessons in *Advanced Business for Social Benefits*.

I believe that the words of Jesus in Matthew 5:14-15 (NKJV) capture this book's perspective very well. To paraphrase His wisdom into the context of this book's topic, I note as follows: *If you set a good example in serving important social needs, your example will increasingly become the way that all those who are affected by and observe what you do will think and act.*

There's an important reminder in 1 Corinthians 13:1-13 (NKJV) for how to direct your efforts in being a good example:

> Though I speak with the tongues of men and of angels, but have not love, I have become sounding brass or a clanging cymbal. And though I have *the gift of* prophecy, and understand all mysteries and all knowledge, and though I have all faith, so that I could remove mountains, but have not love, I am nothing. And though I bestow all my goods to feed *the poor*, and though I give my body to be burned, but have not love, it profits me nothing.
>
> Love suffers long *and* is kind; love does not envy; love does not parade itself, is not puffed up; does not behave rudely, does not seek its own, is not provoked, thinks no evil; does not rejoice in iniquity, but rejoices in the truth; bears all things, believes all things, hopes all things, endures all things.

> Love never fails. But whether *there are* prophecies, they will fail; whether *there are* tongues, they will cease; whether *there is* knowledge, it will vanish away. For we know in part and we prophesy in part. But when that which is perfect has come, then that which is in part will be done away.
>
> When I was a child, I spoke as a child, I understood as a child, I thought as a child; but when I became a man, I put away childish things. For now we see in a mirror, dimly, but then face to face. Now I know in part, but then I shall know just as I also am known.
>
> And now abide faith, hope, love, these three; but the greatest of these is love.

I need some help from you as we think together about lovingly solving major social problems and serving the related needs as a way to increase profits. For the second time in 400 Year Project (documenting ways to accomplish improvements at least 20 times faster with the same or less time, effort, and resources — see the details at www.fastforward400.com) books, I describe methods for achieving a complementary 2,000 percent solution goal whose benefits and processes may not be entirely clear to you as we begin.

In fact, your instincts, your experiences, and what you have read may have focused on just the opposite point of view: Seek profits without considering social impacts unless illegal actions are taking place.

Will you suspend your disbelief, please, while reading this Introduction and the first few lessons? As you keep an open mind, I will develop the case for why this book's goal and related activities can add substantial stakeholder value in conjunction with applying the first five complementary breakthroughs (gaining market share while accelerating market growth by 20 times, reducing stakeholder and company costs of an offering by at least 96 percent, eliminating 96 percent of investment needed to supply offerings, increasing value for all stakeholders by 20 times, and stimulating your organization's innovation by encouraging competitors to innovate and copy) that are discussed in *Business Basics*, *Advanced Business*, and *Advanced Business for Innovation*.

Thank you. I appreciate your openness.

Let me begin by sharing what I have published previously on this subject. The following material is drawn from Chapter 11 of *Adventures of an Optimist* (Mitchell and Company Press, 2007) in which I lay out the case for the exponential-benefit expansions that can follow from organizations combining six complementary breakthroughs (ways of enhancing results by at least 20 times with the same or fewer resources and effort that fully multiply the benefits of one another) to increase stakeholder benefits by over 64 million times:

> Let's poke around among those areas that economists like to complain no one pays any attention to.
>
> What do I mean? Here's an example: The tragedy of the commons is a problem familiar to economists. Provide something for free to everyone, and the privilege will be abused until the common resource all but disappears. In early New England towns, a central area was left open for general use. These town commons would be grazed down to the dirt by farmers' cows and sheep until no one could graze livestock there anymore. It was hard for the commons to be put to recreational use after the farmers were done with them. A similar problem today is the rapidly shrinking stock of fish in the world's oceans. Fishermen make the most by taking as many fish as possible until little of a given species is left. The fishermen move on to another species, reducing the global food supply by permanently depressing fish stocks below what the oceans could support.
>
> Those who study social problems point to air and water pollution, traffic congestion, and overcrowding at free events as examples of the same issue. In studying these problems, scholars are

usually quick to point out that while solving these problems has great value for everyone, there's not enough profit potential to encourage any individual or organization to simply be responsible to the general good.

I have a little secret for you: Those scholars don't seem to know about 2,000 percent solutions. Centuries of pollution and waste have left the world filled with valuable opportunities to fix what is already a mess. A simple example is that many new mining operations don't dig up any ore at all; they simply reprocess the piles of tailings left over from earlier ores that were processed for a different mineral.

One of my students in Asia found that his company could make much more money by going to zero emissions than it could by being a polluter. Why? Waste can be turned into something valuable if you focus on the opportunity. What's more, the same company increases its profits from waste elimination by returning cleaner river water after processing than the water it originally pumped into the plant.

Forecasters are predicting great problems because of steadily reducing supplies of clean water, increasing air pollution coming from developing countries, and great expansion of toxic materials into the soils and buildings of poorer countries (such as carcinogenic chemicals, asbestos, and heavy metals). Clearly the social costs of continuing these trends will be enormous in terms of reduced life spans, disease, and medical care.

Despite the gloomy forecasts, 2,000 percent solutions are undoubtedly available. However, such solutions are highly unlikely to be developed by the least effective organizations, minimally educated people, and weakest governments. Chances are quite good, though, that these problems can be profitably solved by those with know-how for creating 2,000 percent solutions.

Let's go back to the mine example. Even more profit could have been gained initially if a more effective miner had been processing ore from the beginning to extract more types of minerals and leave less waste in piles. What if the world's leading companies in ore processing technology added a business activity to provide outsourcing services to mines for processing ore? Such a company could bid for the right to process the ore from mines, install the latest equipment, and operate in ways that would leave the least amount of waste. Soon, the technology company's size would be more than 20 times larger by adding another line of business that also created enormous social benefits.

Let's update that idea for containing air pollution in China. Major sources of the pollution in that burgeoning country are power plants burning coal and electrical generators using petroleum. All the soot that goes into the air now could, instead, be turned into something profitable either by generating more power from the same fuel or turning the waste into something valuable. Pollution control equipment makers could provide an outsourcing business similar to the one I proposed for ore processing equipment makers to profitably reduce waste. By applying their capital and know-how, large improvements could follow.

My suggestion is that each organization that wants to create more benefits find and operate in ways to profitably reduce the economic costs created by the world's environmental pollutants by 20 times the value of the organization's own profits. Figuring out the numbers might require having access to a few specialists to identify costs. As an example, if air pollution was bad enough in a given location, the pollution might be reducing life expectancy by 10 years. Let's say that the people affected could have earned an extra $100,000 over those 10 years. If 10,000 people live 10 years longer, that improvement would have an economic value of one billion dollars before looking at other benefits such as less need for health care from lung-related ailments. If those same people who live longer are the company's customers for other offerings, another chance to improve an organization's profitable growth is provided.

Why is providing this kind of benefit a good idea when you aren't helping your own customers? Let me explain by beginning with an economist's argument. If you reduce global economic costs by 20 times your current profits, you've just expanded the ability of the world's customers to buy. There's a general increase in purchasing power that benefits everyone. Many people remember that Henry Ford decided to pay his worker's five dollars a day as wages, well above what he needed to pay to keep his costs down. Mr. Ford did this because he realized that he was better off with employees who could afford to buy the cars they made; if other employers followed through on this example, car consumption would be greatly helped. Likewise, if others follow your example, general purchasing power rises further for you and everyone else.

There's also a terrific preference for doing business with companies that reduce harmful pollution and solve other expensive social problems. More customers will seek you out as a result. For companies that directly serve consumers, that preference can be enough to turn you into an industry leader.

In addition, such companies have a much greater ability to attract top talent. Many people would like to work as employees for, be partners with, invest in, or be suppliers to those who are making important improvements. Many idealistic young people will be drawn to larger companies only for this reason, knowing that smaller organizations have potentially less impact in dealing with similar kinds of issues.

Naturally, there's individual self-interest in providing such benefits as well. Do you want to suffer some disease because others have done a poor job of containing harmful materials? I'm sure the answer to that question is "no," so it benefits you personally to become involved in creating more benefits in these ways.

In sharing those perspectives, I built on some assumptions about human nature and the current situation for providing social benefits. Let me spell out five of the most important assumptions:

1. A highly successful organization will tend to do more of the same when expanding its activities. In doing so, leaders can easily begin to focus on smaller and smaller opportunities compared to the organization's size, simply because such opportunities are more easily captured and profited from.
2. Working on huge expansions in benefits from solving social problems can be morally inspiring, enormously energizing, and mentally liberating for those who share a strong desire to provide such benefits.
3. Because business philosophies have so long favored looking for opportunities almost every place except where social benefits will be the greatest, there should be many missed opportunities here, especially on a large scale.
4. Governments often operate activities that provide social benefits. Due to the nature of politics, such engagements can end up being compromised in many ways.
5. The economic value of many social benefits that are too infrequently provided is often a large multiple of the cost to provide the benefits. By providing financing that covers the cost of producing the benefits until such time as the economic value is realized, many more social benefits can be supplied.

I spell out these assumptions, in part, to invite your questions and challenges. Contact me at donmitchell@fastforward400.com/. I also share the assumptions to help you understand that the purpose of serving social benefits is to create more for society, as well as to increase an organization's profits. You may have been surprised that I argue for increasing social benefits by 20 times more than corporate profits. While that relationship might appear to be based on some sort of "do-good" impulse without a firm foundation, the argument is, instead, based on the idea that with so many more benefits being provided compared to the profit earned, it will be easier and more attractive to produce and profit from providing such benefits. I draw that conclusion, in part, based on the realization that many traditionalists will oppose your organization's attempts to provide social benefits while seeking a profit, seeing the two goals as inherently in conflict. I've observed such opposition time and again when public benefits were provided for the first time by profit-seeking organizations. Obviously, then, the more you do to provide social benefits compared to the profits, the fewer people who are going to see there being some sort of harm from mixing social benefits and private profits. Accordingly, you won't experience as many roadblocks and delays in launching and expanding your activities.

Some might be tempted to dismiss such a broad focus on creating social benefits to earn a profit as being based on some form of impractical idealism. While many of those who advocate such a broadening of the benefits from any activity base their thinking solely in what matches some personal concept or increases their emotional comfort, *Advanced Business for Social Benefits: Profit from Serving Social Needs Well* takes different guidance. First, direction comes from God's Word, the Bible. Second, insights into how to apply the Bible's wisdom have been gained from the Holy Spirit concerning the many practical ways that profiting from solving and serving social needs well can be good for everyone. Such increased benefits, in turn, can power virtuous cycles of expanded company capabilities, resources, accomplishments, and benefits for sharing that will multiply the results with each cycle.

To demonstrate these perspectives about gaining profits from serving social needs well, each lesson in this book includes a pertinent selection from the Bible and explains how it applies to stimulating the right behavior and creating vast increases in benefits. The lessons also describe ways that the interests and efforts of companies, their stakeholders, and those who receive benefits can be so complementary, even without an intention to do so, that any improvements will automatically translate into much more effectiveness and benefits for all.

Let me also explain what I mean by "serving social needs well." When experts refer to this term, they usually have some practical dimension or purpose in mind. In ordinary speech, of course, "serving social needs well" also suggests doing something for the public in a high-quality way: desirable effectiveness for many people. In contrast to the first two meanings, we often think of "serving social needs well" as describing what we desire for others to have, regardless of its practical value to them. While this book often overtly focuses on serving material needs, either providing something that increases economic worth or acquiring something that is needed at less cost, the book also advances Biblical values by basing the advice on the perspective of what God sees as "serving social needs well." While we may not know exactly how to measure doing so in God's terms, we should certainly not pay any less attention to advancing it. God's measure, for instance, surely means adding lots of love while providing.

For instance, consider Jesus' words in Matthew 6:24 (NKJV): "No one can serve two masters; for either he will hate the one and love the other, or else he will be loyal to the one and despise the other. You cannot serve God and mammon." (If you aren't familiar with the word *mammon*, it refers in this context to worshiping *riches*, as though they were being personified as a god.) In relating ways to better operate businesses, we should always keep in mind that any such benefits should be directed towards advancing God's Kingdom, rather than some selfish purpose of our own. Otherwise, we will simply be worshiping money rather than God, a great sin. We should see using any money developed in this context as simply a means for accomplishing that most important purpose, God's will. I hope you will apply this information to demonstrate God's greatness to the world and to use the resources He supplies through these methods to glorify Him while serving His purposes.

Other 400 Year Project books contain useful guidance for ways to use resources for God's purposes. If you aren't yet familiar with these books, I suggest that you read some or all of them before or while you read and apply this book. A good starting point is *2,000 Percent Living* (Salvation Press, 2010), which describes how to be 20 times more fruitful for the Lord. If you want do delve deeper into the subject of being fruitful, I also suggest *Help Wanted* (2,000 Percent Living Press, 2011). For those who want to focus on witnessing, I recommend *Witnessing Made Easy* (Jubilee Worship Center Step by Step Press, 2010) and *Ways You Can Witness* (Salvation Press, 2010). For anyone who wants to help make a whole nation more fruitful for the Lord, be sure to read and apply *The 2,000 Percent Nation* (400 Year Project Press, 2012).

As you read about the many ways to increase providing social benefits, you may find it helpful to think about how the knowledge could help with expanding and improving a unified community of believers. Such a reference should increase your focus on making fruitful use of what God provides through these amazing methods, thereby reducing your temptation to use the resources in un-Godly ways.

By implementing the appropriate lessons from *Advanced Business for Social Benefits: Profit from Serving Social Needs* Well in conjunction with the 50 lessons in *Advanced Business for Innovation: Stimulate Competitor Innovation and Copying*, the 50 lessons in *Advanced Business: Exponentially Increase Stakeholder Value,* and the 50 lessons for expanding market growth, slashing costs, and eliminating unnecessary investments in *Business Basics* (400 Year Project Press, 2012), a company can increase benefits for its stakeholders by 64 million or more times.

While some might see these potential gains as either being impossible or not very probable, keep in mind that the for-profit edition of *Excellent Solutions* already provides two improvement processes that can expand stakeholder value by over ten trillion times. In addition, The 400 Year Project has produced immense expansions in benefits through the projects of the many people who have applied its God-directed research.

Business Basics, *Advanced Business*, *Advanced Business for Innovation*, and *Advanced Business for Social Benefits* can also provide helpful perspectives and ideas for applying *Excellent Solution's* astonishing value-expanding processes. For instance, lessons in *Business Basics* and the Advanced Business series can help identify benefit-providing, innovation-encouraging, and value-improving elements for a solution that is developed by applying one of the two *Excellent Solutions* processes.

Let me explain other ways to use *Business Basics*, *Advanced Business*, *Advanced Business for Innovation*, and *Advanced Business for Social Benefits* to create some of the stakeholder benefits of an excellent solution. If any of the six complementary improvements described in *Business Basics* or the three books in the Advanced Business series' lessons is enhanced for a second time with a new complementary 2,000 percent solution, total stakeholder value would expand by 1.28 billion times. By sequentially improving any one of the six complementary dimensions on four different occasions by 20 times each (or improving for a second time any four of the combined six dimensions by 20 times), total stakeholder value would then grow by 10 trillion times. By expanding performance in these six complementary dimensions through the lessons supplied in these books, most for-profit company leaders would be able to design and implement such large value-improving solutions much more rapidly, with reduced effort, and less expensively than by separately developing ten complementary 2,000 percent solutions to gain the same result.

As I discuss in *Adventures of an Optimist*, two other value dimensions that are partially addressed in *Business Basics*, *Advanced Business*, and *Excellent Solutions* can also be used to complement these six value dimensions:

1. Lower the cost of capital by 96 percent.

2. Engage many unemployed or underemployed people in highly productive activities.

Since there are no current plans to write more books for the Advanced Business series, I include here some excerpts from *Adventures of an Optimist* to explain these two value dimensions. We begin with lowering the cost of capital by 96 percent:

> [Reducing] the cost of acquiring the initial and subsequent capital for your business or nonprofit organization by at least 96 percent ... will vastly increase the rate of return you'll earn, expand the amount of capital you can access, and stretch how much of the capital you can afford to spend for other purposes.
>
> Here's an example of how some companies are financed: Many entrepreneurs start up their businesses using personal savings. But along the way, their businesses hit a few bumps in the road, and they run out of money. So the entrepreneurs borrow from friends, family, neighbors, and a mortgage company. Matters are fine for a while. Then the companies hit bigger bumps, and the entrepreneurs need more capital again.
>
> Eyeing the credit card offers that arrive in the mail every day, the entrepreneurs apply for every credit card that crosses the threshold. Most of these initial interest rates are quite low: For transferred balances, the rate may be 0 percent for the first six months.
>
> Then the companies have tiny cash-flow hiccups and are a few weeks late on some credit card payments. The rate of interest on those maxed-out credit cards is immediately adjusted to 26 percent while a 5 percent late fee and a 5 percent overlimit fee are added each month. None of these interest charges and fees is tax-deductible. So every time the owners are late on these credit card payments, the annual charge is going to be over 100 percent a year after tax. If you don't believe me, just add up those 12 per-

cent monthly charges on the increasing balance due for a year and see what number you come up with.

As an alternative way to access capital, most such companies fail to consider how they might use customers and suppliers as low-cost investors. Here's an example: An accounting firm might offer to hold its prices for two years for clients who are willing to pay annual retainers in advance. The accounting firm should do this if it can invest the unused retainer amounts to earn more than the cost of foregone fee increases or to reduce debts that create high interest and fee costs. Why would clients want to do that? Many clients prefer the certainty of keeping expenses under control to the uncertainties of earning what fluctuating near-term interest rates might provide.

Companies on a high-growth trajectory have big capital cost challenges as well. They may feel they need such huge amounts of capital at one time that they have no choice but to access money from venture capitalists. What's the problem? Venture capitalists are looking to make a 45 percent a year return on their investments. Of course, venture capital money works out great if the company flops because the money doesn't have to be repaid. However, if the company is a huge success beyond anyone's expectation, the cost of that capital can be even higher than what the credit card companies get paid under adverse circumstances.

What are some choices? Such a company with high-growth potential can work with prospective customers to slash that cost. For instance, the fledgling firm might approach those potential customers who can be most profitable to serve and help the firm gain the most credibility in the marketplace. If the prospects like what they see, the new company could offer preferred access to technology and exclusive purchase contracts in exchange for options to buy stock. Both companies make much more money that way. In addition, if you borrow money in a currency that's dropping fast enough in value, you have a negative cost of capital. Stay liquid when your equity value temporarily drops, and you can repurchase equity at less than the cost of selling it earlier. The biggest opportunities, however, come in developing the optimal mix of investors. Create an oversupply of eager investors and you'll see your cost of capital plummet. Choosing a great business model that employs exponentially multiplying 2,000 percent solutions is a great first step in creating such an oversupply of eager investors. Good investor research and communications development help, too.

On the nonprofit side, donors are sensitive to how much of the money raised goes for program benefits rather than to solicitations and other overhead expenses. Be very efficient in this performance, and the funds you raise will grow much faster as well. Yet many nonprofits operate for decades before giving any thought to how they can acquire low-cost capital to operate and support their activities.

Let me share with you now some excerpts from *Adventures of an Optimist* about engaging many unemployed or underemployed people in highly productive activities:

> Most of the world's people are desperately poor. Their lack of resources leads to permanent problems. Some babies don't properly develop their brains for lack of a few hundred dollars in nutrients. Lives are ravaged by diseases that are preventable with clean water, inexpensive vaccines, and easy-to-make medicines. Hundreds of millions of people with above-average intellect never receive enough education to develop their minds to anywhere near their full potential. Entrepreneurs capable of leading thousands to economically useful lives lack the investment capital to train and employ those thousands.
>
> What's the root of the problem? It takes a long time and a lot of investment in people before individuals can earn their keep and support others. Short-change the most valuable parts of that time and investment, and the value of the lost potential is an

enormous multiple of the resources that aren't expended in the near term.

Large organizations won't, in most cases, be able to think of ways to earn a near-term profit from solving these problems of helping people achieve their potential. Does that mean we are at the end of opportunities to create more benefits? I don't think so. Other approaches offer potential.

Research conducted by my students in Africa has shown that there are millions of partially able entrepreneurs who can become leaders in creating enormous economic and social progress. How could this potential be turned into a happy result? By establishing a new type of entrepreneurship – enterprises that will profitably employ hundreds of millions of people who now have few prospects for earning much of a living.

How might organizations in developed countries profitably improve the effectiveness of such entrepreneurs? I can see several possibilities; here are a few choices for helping these entrepreneurs:

- Develop new business models that benefit from employing lots of energetic, but undereducated, entrepreneurs. An example is providing such entrepreneurs with opportunities to directly sell your organization's offerings. Direct sellers like Avon are already having success in this regard. Such business models will be more successful, of course, if inexpensive entrepreneurial education is included.

- Partner with underdeveloped entrepreneurs by providing information, training, capital, and support to the partnership while the entrepreneurs supply their efforts, time, and determination. The most successful of such entrepreneurs could later be hired by companies to develop relationships and partnerships with other underdeveloped entrepreneurs. This business model could be especially attractive in delivering technical services where a local language and awareness of local customs are needed in order to be effective. ServiceMaster, for instance, could partner in this way with underdeveloped entrepreneurs to provide excellent cleaning services for restaurants, hotels, and hospitals.

- Establish business models that turn promising employees in poor countries into business owners. Chains of mom 'n pop retailers could provide tryouts for couples to purchase and operate the stores. The resulting chain would be more successful through combining its knowledge, marketing, systems, and purchasing clout.

- Manufacturers could develop modular ways to expand into a country, beginning with making simple, labor-intensive components that are expensive to ship. These production modules could be set up and operated by the manufacturer at first until running smoothly. Later, the production units could be sold to people who work in the enterprise and have done a good job of learning how to lead and operate the production. Customer awareness of the company's efforts to provide local content and ownership would probably assist in selling more of the items in that country.

- Manufacturers could also provide training and licenses to distribute their products in a given country. This approach would be most attractive in sparsely populated locales that present distribution difficulties. To begin, these networks could be focused on selling the simplest items and providing the least valuable replacement parts. Those who did well could eventually be upgraded into establishing authorized repair centers.

- Transportation companies could operate common carriage warehouses where fledgling entrepreneurs who cannot afford facilities could rent secure spaces for valuable items. These warehouses would then benefit from more transportation business being brought to the facility by these entrepreneurs.

- Organizations of all kinds could utilize a policy of emphasizing outsourcing to local entrepreneurs. If nothing else, such a policy would be helpful for those who are educated but don't know much about running businesses to get their feet wet in entrepreneurial ventures. Here's an example: Rather than having their own training departments teach basic literacy and numeracy skills, companies might hire teachers to provide such knowledge and experience during evenings and weekends. Vocational school teachers could be hired to provide various basic technical skills. Hospitals might provide opportunities for their best nurses to train nurse's aides in exchange for additional compensation.

There is an enormous multiplier effect of such activities in uplifting lives. First, the number of gainfully employed grows very rapidly. Of course, most of these people will have low-wage jobs, but that's how economic development usually starts. The holders of those jobs will certainly be better off than before. Second, local purchasing of simple consumer goods expands very rapidly, creating the opportunity for more entrepreneurs to produce and sell those products. Third, you rapidly create a generation of entrepreneurial role models who will inspire others to take this career path. In some underdeveloped countries, it's very unusual now to have such role models. Instead, teens try to learn to be entrepreneurs from other teens who don't know any more than they do. Fourth, the expansion in goods creates a need for much more transportation and storage, which expands the easier entrepreneurial opportunities still further. Fifth, by attracting educated people to be entrepreneurs, you are bound at some point to stimulate the development of low-cost, part-time schools that specialize in preparing entrepreneurs for areas where demand is greatest. For instance, such schools can help reduce enormous shortages of trained leadership and personnel in fields such as plumbing, electrical work, automotive repairs, equipment repairs, and advanced construction. With many more people now earning their livelihoods through trade or manufacturing rather than subsistence farming, larger-scale agriculture can also expand, making it possible to substitute equipment for human work and animal energy. You can expect that the number of people receiving adequate nutrition and education will rapidly increase. Create one successful entrepreneur in a family, and chances are that entrepreneur will find ways to help the rest of the extended family. Make these shifts in ways of doing things across a whole nation, and you reduce the likelihood that during times of drought the country will lack foreign reserves to buy food and medicines. As a result, overall health, knowledge, productivity, and wealth will improve on a sustainable basis.

Are there any other complementary dimensions that a for-profit company can use as performance enhancements for greatly expanding stakeholder benefits? Yes, I believe that there are many more than just the two dimensions I've just discussed. I list here two more:

1. Invest in upgrading the skills, knowledge, and resources of many underdeveloped people, especially those with little education and experience, so they can make maximum contributions to all stakeholders and then continue operating in partnership with those who can, as a result, accomplish still more. This approach would work best after a foundation is laid by engaging many underutilized people (such as those who are unemployed or underemployed) in highly productive activities.
2. Redirect the public's agenda, attention, and resources into improving or increasing highly valuable activities and resources at little cost.

Feel free to add any other complementary performance dimensions that you prefer.

Let me also remind you that while this book is about for-profit businesses, aspects of the discussions about serving social needs well are equally, if not more, applicable to nonprofit organizations.

If you have questions or would like to discuss any of these subjects, donmitchell@fastforward400.com is my e-mail address.

Now, back to the book at hand. The lessons in this book primarily concern the following topics:

1. Selecting benefits to provide
2. Developing and adjusting stakeholder relationships
3. Launching such a program

Because the discussions of these topics are interwoven in the lessons, the book is not formally separated into different parts. Instead, the lessons are presented in an order that will help you best understand what needs to be done.

I encourage you to direct your colleagues to those lessons that are most relevant to their responsibilities. Doing so will make it easier to redirect your organization's activities in the most fruitful ways.

To make such referrals of colleagues easier for you, I briefly describe each of the book's lessons here. Lesson One examines more closely the reasons why greatly increasing social benefits can also be helpful for expanding company profits. The lesson concludes by outlining some steps to take for beginning to identify which social benefits to provide.

In Lesson Two, we look closely at current and potential customers to identify ways that your business model should be revised to solve social problems and serve social needs well in ways that will increase your attractiveness to purchasers. We see that customers hold the key to most of the potential advantages for an organization from serving social needs well.

For many organizations, end users of offerings are seen much more dimly and imperfectly than are customers. Consequently, Lesson Three encourages gaining insights from how end users react to changes in your business model that enable providing more social benefits.

In Lesson Four, we consider ways that suppliers can enhance providing social benefits well while also helping you attract more customers, end users, and other supporters of your activities. If current suppliers aren't able to do what's needed, finding and developing new suppliers can be necessary.

Employees are the focus of Lesson Five. We consider their critical importance in finding solutions for pressing social problems and effectively increasing the provision of scarce benefits. Much of your credibility in achieving your purpose will be determined by how well employees go about such important work.

Lesson Six concentrates on employees' families as a source of encouragement for employees, stakeholders, and those who might decide to become stakeholders. Such families' comments are often taken more seriously than what a respected "objective" source might say about your organization's activities to supply more social benefits. In this lesson, we also consider the importance of limiting negative comments by employees' families that can create skepticism concerning the company and its efforts.

Owners have more influence over what an organization does than do many other stakeholders. In Lesson Seven, we focus on the kinds of non-economic advantages provided to owners by seeking to greatly grow social benefits as a means of expanding company profits. During the lesson, we also allude to establishing the credibility of a solution before asking owners to support it, as well as the significance of succeeding for expanding owners' value in the company.

Lesson Eight considers working with dream-team (ideal) partners to accomplish results that none of the organizations could achieve on their own. In the lesson, we consider how to identify the ideal partners and what relationship to have with each one.

Adding different types of distributors can increase the efficiency and effectiveness of providing social benefits and earning profits by doing so, the topic of Lesson Nine. In this lesson, we consider how the Grameen-Danone joint venture and Aravind Eye Care System were able to accomplish more with this approach. You will also receive directions for how to gain even more advantages from adding different types of distributors than other organizations have.

In Lesson Ten, we explore the potential to attract unpaid volunteers to perform tasks that might otherwise be done by employees and suppliers for pay. While nonprofit organizations have often relied on this approach, too few for-profit organizations with appealing social practices have done so. We explore how to go far beyond the state of the art in this regard.

Strangers are too often ignored as a potential resource for accomplishing more in providing social benefits. Due to the appeal of your purpose, those who have had no more contact with your activities than hearing about what you are doing can become valuable contributors by sharing their reactions to what you are doing with others, performing a short-term task, and providing valuable information. Lesson Eleven explores what kinds of cooperation to seek from interested strangers and how to gain such assistance.

In Lesson Twelve, we consider how being a good example by providing more social benefits can lead competitors to take complementary actions to expand such benefits. This lesson draws extensively on concepts contained in *Advanced Business for Innovation*.

Every organization affects the communities in which it operates. Lesson Thirteen considers how to positively engage with such communities to increase the social benefits that are received, as well as improve profits.

Lesson Fourteen focuses on how companies should recast how they interact with governments to seek ways to provide benefits for governments and to gain support that multiplies the results from the companies' own efforts. This topic is expanded in later lessons.

Experts can become very valuable contributors to a company's social-benefit expansion by adding experience, knowledge, and credibility. However, such experts must first become interested in what you intend and then become willing to contribute. Helping you appreciate the potential roles of such experts is explored in Lesson Fifteen.

Lesson Sixteen addresses how to engage authorities to gain support for your solution. Authorities differ from experts in being able to influence large numbers of stakeholders, regardless of their skill and knowledge in the subject area. For instance, a popular president of the United States might influence many people to engage in an activity without knowing much about how to accomplish the goal. Franklin Delano Roosevelt's support for the March of Dimes is an example.

Experts and authorities aren't the only useful sources of public support. Foundations can also make an important difference in similar ways, while also being able to supply financial resources to fund experiments, sustain support during lean times, and multiply the social benefits that are supplied. This is our topic in Lesson Seventeen.

In Lesson Eighteen, we look at our last and largest potential group of contributors, the general public. From among those who don't yet know what you are doing and have no connection to current stakeholders can come most of your new stakeholders. With enough of such people, you will gain sufficient added support for your organization's activities to greatly increase the social benefits you can provide and enhance your company's profits.

We look next at establishing a foundation for an irresistible cause. The March of Dimes is our example, from which we develop tests to be applied for ascertaining the appeal of the various kinds of social benefits you could profitably increase. The assignments in Lesson Nineteen involve rethinking the fifth assignment of Lesson One.

Lesson Twenty focuses on learning more about how to attract attention for and support of your irresistible cause, so that the social benefits you plan to increase will be expanded as much as possible due to the support of stakeholders and the general public. In doing so, stay focused on what the Bible and the Holy Spirit direct.

After that, we develop compelling stories to attract interest, support, and action for the irresistible cause. To the extent that the stories can be based on advancing God's Kingdom, the stories will be more persuasive. This dual intent is discussed in Lesson Twenty-One.

In Lesson Twenty-Two, we explore ways to hold an unmistakable launch event for attracting attention to and support for your irresistible cause. The lesson is complementary to one in *Business Basics* about market expansion through holding one momentous event.

Cheerful givers are loved by God. In Lesson Twenty-Three, we look at ways to increase commitment for supporting the irresistible cause.

Lesson Twenty-Four focuses on effectively increasing commitment through providing experiences that many people can share and feel touched by. In so doing, the original ways that commitment was built will need to be expanded and streamlined.

With much of such commitment in place, it's time to train committed people to perform the key tasks the irresistible cause requires. We explore how to perform such training in Lesson Twenty-Five.

With Lesson Twenty-Six, we start developing a second way of advancing social benefits by 400 times: replacing a government activity. While the opportunity is large, the potential opposition can be even greater. In this lesson, we look at preliminary steps for creating a foundation to install such a replacement.

Another way to replace a government activity is to demonstrate the value of governments providing financing for beneficiaries. With access to such funds, beneficiaries can then choose to purchase social benefits that you provide more efficiently and effectively than the government through your complementary 2,000 percent solution. We discuss examples of ways to engage in such replacements in Lesson Twenty-Seven.

Lesson Twenty-Eight is a counterpart to Lesson Twenty-Seven by looking, instead, at using private financing to fund greatly expanding the provision of social benefits.

In the third lesson on the role of financing for replacing a government activity, we consider in Lesson Twenty-Nine directly providing such financing. In this way, beneficiaries can be better protected from harm.

In Lesson Thirty, we look, instead, at replacing a government activity by teaching beneficiaries how to finance themselves. As in lessons twenty-eight and twenty-nine, we consider the example of Dr. Donald R. Kamdonyo's activities in developing entrepreneurs in Malawi to discuss the possibilities of how such an approach might be successfully accomplished.

In the book's final four lessons, we examine a third strategy for expanding social benefits by more than 400 times and profits by at least 20 times in doing so: replacing private enterprise activities, whether by nonprofit or for-profit organizations. The subject opens with a few examples in Lesson Thirty-One.

Lesson Thirty-Two looks at replacing private-enterprise activities that have high social costs. In this lesson, we develop an example of helping the newly employed obtain lower-cost transportation.

We then turn to looking at private-enterprise activities that provide few social benefits. Our example is cigarette manufacturing, marketing, and distribution. Lesson Thirty-Three considers ways that a new business could be established for encouraging smokers to redirect their spending for tobacco into providing social benefits, instead.

In Lesson Thirty-Four, we close our investigation of replacing private-enterprise activities by considering the opportunity to improve any business whose social benefits can be directly increased by more than a hundred times. Building on a base of the effects from the expanded direct benefits, the combined direct and indirect benefits will usually expand by at least 400 times.

In the Afterword, I conclude with some comments about the path you've been on and your next steps.

By the time you finish reading *Advanced Business for Social Benefits*, your understanding of what it means to "do business" will have permanently become much more fruitful. You will appreciate many new ways your company can effectively address long-standing, public problems, as well as increase the benefits that your stakeholders receive. In the process, you'll come to see solving social problems and supplying large amounts of social benefits as a spiritually rewarding calling. Shifting to this approach will add spiritual dimensions to managing a business. You will also delight in receiving the support of many new people and be encouraged to have so many helpers.

Be sure to read the Appendix One, as well, where I describe my Christian experiences and testimony. Feel free to share this information with anyone you feel would benefit from learning about how God has touched and improved my life.

In Appendix Two, I include brief profiles of some of the organizations discussed in the lessons.

While all the covers for books produced by The 400 Year Project contain images designed to reinforce the books' messages, you may have a little harder time understanding this book's image than those of the previously published books. The birds you see are puffins living in Maine, the results of a remarkable project to restore these sea birds to this habitat after hunters had killed their predecessors many decades earlier. The project has not only restored these fascinating birds to some of their old territory, the work has also shown how to restore rare and displaced sea birds worldwide. These birds are social in ways that remind some of people, and puffins depend on a confluence of favorable conditions in the environment to survive and thrive, much as at-risk humans do. Thus, these puffins are a metaphor for the potential benefits from performing the many unfilled tasks of serving social needs well. You can read more about this work in *Project Puffin* (Yale University Press, 2015) by Stephen W. Kress and Derrick Z. Jackson.

Let's now begin with Lesson One and consider the selection of benefits to provide.

Lesson One

Benefit Selection

"You did not choose Me, but I chose you and
appointed you that you should go and bear fruit,
and that *your fruit should remain,*
that whatever you ask the Father in My name
He may give you."

— John 15:16 (NKJV)

In John 15:16 (NKJV), Jesus tells His disciples at the Last Supper about what is to come. The Bible also teaches that before we were born God developed a plan for each of our lives, a plan that will expand His Kingdom. To help us accomplish this plan, the Holy Spirit draws all people to Jesus. Those who accept Jesus as their Lord and Savior then are filled with the Holy Spirit, which begins a transformation that continues throughout life on Earth into becoming more like Jesus. The Holy Spirit then softens our hearts to desire what God wants. Our prayers are also empowered by the Spirit to enable us to accomplish our part of fulfilling these desires. So keep these resources in mind as you consider what benefits to provide. God will supply what you cannot imagine or do on your own.

Solving difficult social problems to greatly increase social benefits and expand company profits will seem to some like a strange way to run a business. The traditional view has been that focusing on anything other than increasing profits and shareholder value simply serves to distract and hobble a company. Let's look at that view more carefully.

In the last fifty years, a new type of organization has developed that some people refer to as a *social enterprise*, an organization that seeks to expand social benefits as its main mission. Some of such organizations are nonprofits, while others seek to earn money. Profits, if sought, are thought to be simply a necessary part of developing enough resources to provide the social benefits.

Examples of such enterprises include the Grameen Bank (microlending, education for the poor, and venture capital for the poor headquartered in Bangladesh), Aravind Eye Care System (a world leader in low-cost eye care for the poor headquartered in India), the Grameen-Danone dairy products joint venture (a social enterprise engaged in improving health, economic security, and self-esteem in Bangladesh), Newman's Own (a nonprofit grocery products company based in the United States), and the many nonprofit microlenders that seek to fund small farmers and entrepreneurs around the world to lift living standards. A brief description of these organizations can be found in materials quoted from each organization's Web site in Appendix Two.

More recently, a new type of social enterprise has entered the scene: one that seeks to provide social benefits as its primary goal but that also isn't shy about earning whatever profits it can from being a reliable provider of valuable social benefits. RECYCLA Chile (based in Chile) is an example of such an enterprise.

As its name suggests, RECYCLA Chile recycles materials that others don't want. In this case, the company specializes in electronic gear and components, especially the sort that was never intended to reach landfills where the soil can be poisoned by such material. While numerous organizations claim to recycle, many of them simply send waste to third world countries where it ends up in landfills, thus exporting pollution rather than avoiding it.

RECYCLA Chile is different in that it seeks to do the best possible job of recycling such material. While its waste customers actually pay the company to take the material away, many of its competitors, instead, pay for this valuable waste. In turn, RECYCLA Chile certifies its customers for having followed good practices, so that their customers can be aware that proper recycling is being done.

To do so, RECYCLA Chile sorts out what can be repaired or reused. Those materials are provided to poor people. What can't be reused that way is treated to separate out the most usable metals and minerals. For what is most difficult to treat properly, RECYCLA Chile hires the world's top specialists to do the necessary work.

For its own staff, RECYCLA Chile relies as much as possible on former prisoners who have been released and are seeking to live as upright citizens. Many customers are attracted to the idea that the company in a sense "recycles" some of its employees from the scrap heap of public censure so they can earn an honest living.

When entrepreneurs set out to accomplish new kinds of goals, one of the few things you can be certain of is that they will have unexpected results. While many people thought that social enterprises would lose a fortune and need to be bailed out by donors or the bankruptcy courts, some social enterprises (such as the ones I've mentioned) have, in fact, turned out to be amazingly profitable.

Consider the nonprofit Newman's Own. The organization provides food and beverage products to supermarkets and restaurants. To maximize its ability to generate cash, no equity is retained. All operations are funded solely with debt that is totally repaid to lenders once a year. Whatever cash remains is then donated to a foundation that distributes the money to various charitable causes. So far, over $400 million has been contributed from cash-based earnings.

Can you imagine Coca-Cola operating that way? Or McDonald's? Probably not. Interestingly enough, McDonald's is a major customer for Newman's Own coffee and salad dressings.

These unexpected profits and growth for Newman's Own first attracted attention from business scholars and entrepreneurs. Later, competitors began to study what was going on, as well.

To date, a number of factors contributing to high profitability and growth have been identified. While I've read widely in this literature, I'm sure I've missed some important cases. I also suspect that many potential sources of high profitability have not yet been employed ... and those opportunities remain fallow for now. We'll look into such opportunities in future lessons.

Consumer-products companies were the first to notice that some consumers will select one offering over another if everything is equal except the providers' contributions to increasing social benefits. In such cases, the organization that is known for making a bigger social contribution will almost always make the sale.

Traditionally, many organizations sought to cash in on this phenomenon by allocating a small portion of profits to a foundation that funded highly visible public activities of which most people approved. Companies often thought of this spending as simply an alternative way of marketing their offerings. For instance, Philip Morris (now Altria), the cigarette giant, dominated high-profile art museum shows around the world for decades, which many people viewed as a sort of "sin" tax to atone for some of its harm to public health. Such activities ceased to provide much marketing benefit at some point in the last few decades, and most such funds were, instead, directed by big companies into public activities that indirectly helped the firm ... such as by improving public education of the sort needed by hard-to-hire entry-level employees.

Where public consciousness is high, end users will sometimes pay a premium for products that reflect their values about social benefits. Fair Trade coffee is an example in the United States. Purchasers of such coffee pay higher prices for their beans so that farmers and farm workers are lifted out of extreme poverty and can afford to use more environmentally friendly practices.

Corporations are often even bigger payers of premiums, reflecting their greater ability to appreciate the full impact of whatever social benefits are being supplied. For instance, those who dispose of electronic junk with RECYCLA Chile pay for its removal while most recyclers pay the source of valuable junk to haul it away. Poisoning of landfills is reduced ... and RECYCLA's customers obtain the right to use a seal that identifies them to their own customers as more considerate recyclers of electronic waste. Presumably, these RECYCLA Chile customers gain some benefit in selling more products of their own and in recruiting employees and suppliers who share their values.

In highly competitive industries, employers may have to compete by making their work more desirable than what others do. The chance to provide social benefits is increasingly such a competitive device for gaining and retaining top-performing employees.

Before listing the potential ways that social benefits can increase company profits or nonprofit financial resources, let me also mention that providing more social benefits can also bring cost and investment reductions. For example, people may volunteer their time rather than needing to be paid (as occurs with the lending groups that do much of the administrative work for the Grameen Bank). Because of strong desires to provide more social benefits, people in the organization may work harder, do more to improve productivity, and accept lower pay and less desirable working conditions (as occurs with the Aravind Eye Care System).

I also find that the desire to enormously increase social benefits seems to inspire better than usual business-model innovation. It's as though having a purpose of increasing social benefits makes leaders more sensitive to the needs and interests of the stakeholders whom they should always be faithfully serving.

Some such organizations are greatly helped by subsidies from governments, donors, and affiliated organizations wishing to launch, expand, or sustain social-benefit increases. Increasingly, philanthropists and public companies are looking for ways to do so.

Ultimately, having provided the social benefits can lead to satisfied beneficiaries who share the good news with others who become more willing to interact with and cooperate with the social enterprise. Those who receive free eye surgeries at the Aravind Eye Care System hospitals return to their villages and neighborhoods singing the organization's praises. These former patients often recruit and accompany other prospects to receive their own examinations and subsequent surgeries, saving Aravind the cost of reaching out to these people.

Let me simplify these observations into nine opportunities:

1. Attract more customers and purchases because of customers wanting to support the social purpose.
2. Obtain premium pricing due to the strength of customer desire to support the social purpose or to the marketing benefits received.
3. Reduce costs by receiving volunteer help or reduced charges from suppliers who favor the purpose for the increased social benefits.
4. Experience fewer costs due to a higher drive among employees, partners, and suppliers for productivity, willingness to work harder in less favorable conditions, and demanding less in payments and benefits.
5. Avoid investments due to stakeholders doing more of such required investing.
6. Increase sensitivity to improving cash flow by all stakeholders because of its effect on providing more for those who receive social benefits.
7. Encourage innovative business models that build on the trust and preference for providing and receiving the social benefits.
8. Potentially receive subsidies from various stakeholders to pay for launching, expanding, or sustaining the benefit provision.
9. Directly create more demand for the firm's offerings due to the resulting social benefits.

For profits to grow by another 20 times, it will be necessary to obtain advantages from as many of these nine categories of potential company benefits as possible. In addition, it will be highly desirable to develop and engage in new categories of advantages.

Also, realize that the more social benefits expand, the easier it will be to achieve the profit-expansion target. Thus, producing 8,000 times more social benefits will do more for profits than stopping at 400 times.

Although it's more of a judgment call than something you can accurately calculate, the more valuable the social benefits are that your organization increases, the greater are the likely positive effects on your organization and its profits. For instance, keeping older people from becoming permanently blind with cataracts adds enormous quality to lives that anyone can appreciate, as well as direct economic benefits that are probably worth tens of thousands of dollars over the remainder of a lifetime.

The more emotionally appealing the social benefits are to all types of stakeholders, the greater, too, will be the potential profit impacts.

In the assignments below, I provide questions designed to help you begin to select the social benefits that your organization should seek to multiply by at least 400 times.

What's the key lesson? *An organization that sincerely wants to accelerate its profitable growth can be helped by expanding the current level of social benefits being provided by a much larger (more than 20 times) multiple of the profit increases that it gains from providing these social benefits.*

Your Lesson One Assignments

1. List the social benefits that you believe your organization could increase by 400 times relative to the current level at a fairly modest cost within two years.

2. Evaluate each such social benefit in terms of its potential to provide profit-increasing benefits through each of the nine categories listed in this lesson.

3. Tentatively identify the social benefits that you could increase the most in percentage terms.

4. Tentatively identify the social benefit that you could increase the most in absolute terms.

5. Consider how motivating providing these social-benefit increases would be for your stakeholders.

6. Next, start from your biggest profit-improvement opportunities, as you understand them today, to evaluate how your business model should be changed to make profitable improvements for providing the social benefits you identified in assignments 3 and 4.

Lesson Two

Evaluate Customer Focus

Then Saul, still breathing threats and murder
against the disciples of the Lord,
went to the high priest and asked letters
from him to the synagogues of Damascus,
so that if he found any who were of the Way,
whether men or women,
he might bring them bound to Jerusalem.

As he journeyed he came near Damascus, and
suddenly a light shone around him from heaven.

Then he fell to the ground, and
heard a voice saying to him,
"Saul, Saul, why are you persecuting Me?"

And he said, "Who are You, Lord?"

Then the Lord said, "I am Jesus,
whom you are persecuting.
It is *hard for you to kick against the goads."*

So he, trembling and astonished, said,
"Lord, what do You want me to do?"

Then the Lord said *to him, "Arise and go into the city,*
and you will be told what you must do."

And the men who journeyed with him
stood speechless, hearing a voice but seeing no one.

Then Saul arose from the ground, and
when his eyes were opened he saw no one.

But they led him by the hand and
brought him *into Damascus.*

And he was three days without sight,
and neither ate nor drank.

— Acts 9:1-9 (NKJV)

Acts 9:1-9 (NKJV) recounts one of the most dramatic examples of changing perspective. Prior to meeting Jesus on the road to Damascus, Saul of Tarsus was a committed opponent of Jesus and His followers. By just one encounter with Jesus and three days to think it over, Saul was transformed into a follower of Jesus, one who became a great missionary to the Gentiles. Similarly, you need to see customers with a new perspective if you are to succeed in greatly increasing the supply of social benefits in profitable ways.

For profits to grow by another 20 times, it will be necessary to obtain advantages from as many as possible of the nine categories of company benefits described in Lesson One. In addition, it will be highly desirable to develop and engage in securing new categories of advantages.

As I mention in Lesson One, realize that the more social benefits expand, the easier it will be to achieve the profit-expansion target. Thus, producing 8,000 times more social benefits will do more for profits than stopping at a 400-times increase.

At the end of Lesson One, you found assignments designed to help you tentatively identify the social benefits you could increase the most that would have the biggest effects on expanding profits. In this lesson, we build on what you learned from that work. If you haven't done that lesson's assignments yet, please do so now before continuing with this lesson.

In the previous lesson, you considered profit impacts mostly in terms of how you operate your business now. Only in the final assignment in that lesson were you asked to consider changes in your business model. In this lesson, we do more work on this assignment:

> *Next, start from your biggest profit-improvement opportunities, as you understand them today, to evaluate how your business model should be changed to make profitable improvements for providing the social benefits you identified in assignments 3 and 4.*

Customer focus is an important aspect of answering this question because customers provide the key to so many of the potential company benefits including these seven:

1. Attract more customers and purchases because of customers wanting to support the social purpose.
2. Obtain premium pricing due to the strength of customer desire to support the social purpose or to the marketing benefits received.
3. Avoid investments due to stakeholders doing more of such required investing.
4. Increase sensitivity to improving cash flow by all stakeholders because of its effect on providing more for those who receive social benefits.
5. Encourage innovative business models that build on the trust and preference for providing and receiving the social benefits.
6. Potentially receive subsidies from various stakeholders to pay for launching, expanding, or sustaining the benefit provision.

7. Directly create more demand for the firm's offerings due to the resulting social benefits.

Let me address each of these points separately, starting with attracting more customers and purchases because of their wanting to support the social purpose. While many businesspeople will think of this potential company benefit in terms of gaining market share, there's a second dimension that can be even more important in underdeveloped markets: bringing in new categories of customers simply due to the social-benefit expansion.

Obviously, such market expansion would be highly desirable by increasing sales because of a faster-growing market, as well as a growing market share. In terms of achieving such a desirable result, it's often important to fine tune which social benefits are increased in order to enhance your appeal to new classes of customers. Doing so may require research and testing with potential customers.

In this respect, RECYCLA Chile's customer-certification program comes to mind. Its customers use this program to assure their customers that all electronic waste is being recycled in the most responsible ways. Without providing such information, undoubtedly some major RECYCLA Chile customers would have continued using less electronic recycling, as well as other less desirable practices. This innovation substantially increased sales for RECYCLA Chile *and* the industry.

For obtaining more premium pricing, providing more valuable benefits or increasing existing benefits will usually be necessary. The certification program at RECYCLA Chile again comes to mind. A great deal of the firm's ability to charge so much more for recycling appears to be based on the value its customers gain from being able to certify to the customers' customers that they are using the best recycling techniques, thereby increasing sales and profits for RECYCLA Chile's customers.

Because RECYCLA Chile's customers value the certification, they pay the company to take the electronic refuse rather than selling it to RECYCLA Chile, as other firms do with their electronic waste. As a consequence, RECYCLA Chile's investments were reduced. Undoubtedly, this willingness to cooperate also influenced customers to incur more of the investment costs for themselves.

Although the concept of certification is far from new, its application to electronic recycling in Chile certainly was. So this business-model innovation was an important part of the firm's success in increasing social benefits by a substantial multiple and its own profits by a smaller, but significant, one.

RECYCLA Chile is also subsidized by some of its workers, the ex-convicts who had difficulty finding honest work, receiving low pay for difficult, unpleasant work. This aspect of the business model ("recycling people") also appealed to the firm's customers, who may be willing to pay a bit more for being able to participate in providing this social benefit, as well.

If RECYCLA Chile's customers saw that their own sales and profits increased enough by providing more social benefits in Chile, some of its customers may well have pressured their suppliers to also use the firm as a way to expand benefits.

The only customer-driven profit opportunity that's missing is for RECYCLA Chile to use the increased social benefits to drive more sales and profits. However, this missing element from RECYCLA Chile's approach is clearly present in the Aravind Eye Care System. Those who receive free and low-cost surgeries often become evangelists encouraging others to use Aravind for eye examinations, treatments, and surgeries that reduce costs and attract more paying customers. Because the first person in a family had been treated for free may have increased the family's disposable income, others in the family could become paying patients.

Particularly in business-model innovations, you need to be open to the idea of adding other categories of social benefits that appeal to major groups of potential customers, as well as to those who purchase from competitors. The hiring of ex-convicts is such an example for RECYCLA Chile. Providing more kinds of social benefits is especially important in instances where there is no single social-benefit expansion that's highly valuable and desired by all those customers you wish to attract.

What's the key lesson? *An organization that sincerely wants to accelerate its profitable growth can be helped by expanding the current level of social benefits by a much larger (more than 20 times) multiple than the profit increases that it seeks to gain from providing these social benefits in ways that reflect changing its customer focus to become more appealing.*

Your Lesson Two Assignments

1. Identify how increasing social benefits could attract many more new purchasers to your organization and to the industry.

2. Evaluate how each social-benefit increase would affect each of the nine categories of potential sales and profit increases listed in Lesson One in terms of existing and potential customers.

3. Measure and consider how other social benefits could be increased to greatly expand the number of new customers gained and profits earned from serving them.

4. Search other industries to find practices that could be brought into your industry for greatly expanding the value of your social-benefit increases to current and potential customers.

5. Test your possible adjustments to providing social benefits with the current and potential customers you wish to attract before shifting what you do.

Lesson Three

Adjust End-User Focus

So then faith comes *by hearing,*
and hearing by the word of God.

But I say, have they not heard? Yes indeed:

"Their sound has gone out to all the earth,
And their words to the ends of the world."

— Romans 10:17-18 (NKJV)

Romans 10:17-18 (NKJV) reminds us that building faith in God requires hearing His Word, an important reason why we are directed by the Bible to share our faith. Similarly, we can't limit our thinking about new business models to what we learn from current and potential customers. We must also look past those purchasers to ascertain the impact on the end users of our current offerings from serving various social needs well.

In Lesson Two, we built on Lesson One's work by evaluating your customer focus to find more valuable ways to provide social benefits well. In doing so, I pointed out how almost all elements of providing more social benefits need to be filtered through considering how customers would respond.

In the course of making such an evaluation, many organizations will do a fine job of considering customers ... while many others will miss major opportunities by failing to fully consider the perspectives of end users, those who ultimately put offerings and social benefits to use. Such missed opportunities are often associated with having myopic customers who pay too little attention to end users of offerings and don't know how end users will respond to expanding social benefits in various ways. Don't forget how important it is not to take the responses of any end users for granted.

In doing so, let me be sure you understand the distinction between the end users of offerings and the end users of social benefits. The former are those who directly employ the offerings your company sells while the latter are those whose lives are most affected by the expanded social benefits. In some cases, the same people will be both types of end users. More often, however, end users will belong to just one of the two groups.

In the case of RECYCLA Chile, anyone who uses some of the materials the company has recycled is an end user of its offerings. Anyone who avoids being poisoned because the waste materials are more judiciously handled is an end user of the social benefits. Notice that the latter group may be much larger or smaller than the former group. Be sure you focus on both types of end users in considering how increasing social benefits in quantity and value will affect your organization's profits. I emphasize this point because it's certainly possible to greatly increase social benefits while either reducing organizational profits or leaving them unchanged.

Let me discuss how end users' reactions to various ways of increasing social benefits can help or hurt the provision of those benefits and the level of an organization's profits along the lines of the nine dimensions I list in Lesson One:

1. Attract more customers and purchases because of customers wanting to support the social purpose.

   As we explored through the RECYCLA Chile example in Lesson Two, many customers will increase purchases because their own customers will buy more due to the social-benefit expansion. Ultimately, such a chain of increased consumption flows from changes in end-user behavior. Thus, an environmentally conscious youngster who requests a first computer as a gift may specify a brand after learning that the manufacturer does better recycling in Chile through RECYCLA Chile.

If, however, RECYCLA Chile adopts some practice that the environmentally conscious youngster doesn't like, the request for a computer may be phrased in terms of not buying from anyone who recycles with RECYCLA Chile.

From this simple example, do you see how end-user behavior affecting purchases determines whether increasing social benefits affects RECYCLA Chile's volume from its customers?

On the social-benefit side of the end-user equation, you can see that such a Chilean youngster who uses an offering is probably also a beneficiary as an end user of the social benefits by not being poisoned with tainted runoff from landfills.

2. Obtain premium pricing due to the strength of customer desire to support the social purpose or to the marketing benefits received.

The strength of end-user feelings and type of actions taken based on preferences for what is being done to create or to add social benefits affect premium pricing even more than the quantity of purchases. That's because purchases are probably unaffected across a broad range of providing more social benefits after reaching some threshold, while only at the highest levels of emotion is a willingness triggered to pay a premium price. Consequently, the type and level of feelings are more important for influencing end users of offerings than for affecting end users of benefits.

3. Reduce costs by receiving volunteer help or reduced charges from suppliers who favor the purpose for the increased social benefits.

   Such volunteers are likely to come from among end users of offerings and social benefits who strongly support what an organization is doing. Suppliers are likewise influenced, in part, by the strength of support they see among social-benefit end users ... especially any they know. The more types of appealing end users who are provided with scarce, valuable social benefits, the greater will be the company's ability to draw this kind of support.

4. Experience fewer costs due to a higher drive among employees, partners, and suppliers for productivity, willingness to work harder in less favorable conditions, and demanding less in payments and benefits.

   When there's great sympathy for social-benefit end users and those who work for and support the organization see the end users being greatly helped by the increased social benefits, desire will obviously grow to help in any way possible. Consider how many adults would respond strongly to the idea of fewer children being poisoned by electronic waste in ways that permanently harm their brains. Almost any parent, grandparent, aunt, or uncle would be strongly moved to help.

5. Avoid investments due to stakeholders doing more of such required investing.

   If stakeholders see that their investments can increase social benefits they care about to end users who stir their emotions by more than any other action they can take, many such stakeholders will be happy to make investments that efficiently contribute to such overall social-benefit gains. Where the offering and social-benefit end users are the same people, the appeal to stakeholders will be even greater.

6. Increase sensitivity to improving cash flow by all stakeholders because of its effect on providing more for those who receive social benefits.

   In most cases of providing more social benefits to end users, the need is far greater than the ability to meet the need. If there's sympathy for these end users and an accurate understanding of how changing cash flow increases or reduces providing social benefits, many stakeholders will again follow paths that increase cash flow and desirable social benefits for end users ... especially if they have few other efficient ways to contribute to providing more of these social benefits.

7. Encourage innovative business models that build on the trust and preference for providing and receiving the social benefits.

   Again, sympathy for the social-benefit end users and honest desires to provide more of these social benefits will keep many people strongly motivated to find more and better ways to deliver the desirable social benefits.

8. Potentially receive subsidies from various stakeholders to pay for launching, expanding, or sustaining the benefit provision.

   Where governments and organizations have strong stakes in end users receiving more social benefits, such subsidies may be the most efficient way for governments and organizations to contribute to accomplishing more in this regard. Sometimes the offering end users will be willing to provide such subsidies, as well.

9. Directly create more demand for the firm's offerings due to the resulting social benefits.

   If the social-benefit end users aren't employing or benefiting from the increased social benefits, this potential company benefit won't occur. The more that end users benefit (both in how many benefits are provided and how beneficial each one is), the greater the effects will be of this dynamic. For example, when the Grameen Bank made a major commitment to enabling access to cellular telephones in Bangladesh for poor women and farmers, the bank unleashed a great wave of prosperity that further expanded demand for low-cost cellular telephones and services. In most cases, these effects will be strongest where offering and social-benefit end users are often the same people.

What's the key lesson? *An organization that sincerely wants to accelerate its profitable growth can be helped by expanding the current level of social benefits by a much larger (more than 20 times) multiple than the profit increases that it gains from providing the social benefits in ways that improve offering and social-benefit end users' circumstances and perceptions of the value of these benefits.*

Your Lesson Three Assignments

1. Identify how increasing the quantity and types of social benefits could attract many more customers and offering and social-benefit end users, and more visible support from them for your organization's activities.

2. Evaluate how each social-benefit increase would affect each of the nine categories of potential sales and profit increases listed in this and the prior two lessons in terms of attracting and obtaining more support from existing and new stakeholders who aren't end users.

3. Search other industries to find practices that could be brought into your industry to greatly expand the value of your social-benefit increases to current and potential end users of offerings and social benefits.

4. Test your potential adjustments for their effects on the current and potential offering and social-benefit end users you wish to serve.

Lesson Four

Select Suppliers

Now may He who supplies seed to the sower,
and bread for food, supply and multiply the seed
you have sown *and increase the fruits of your righteousness,*
while you are *enriched in everything for all liberality,*
which causes thanksgiving through us to God.

– 2 Corinthians 9:10-11 (NKJV)

In 2 Corinthians 9:10-11 (NKJV), we are reminded that God is the ultimate supplier of all the things we use, whether personally or in our businesses. That reminder is timely for this lesson in which we consider the right way to select suppliers: We should choose suppliers who seek to apply His righteousness in helping us provide for more social needs.

Let me first discuss how selection of suppliers can help or hurt providing those benefits and expanding an organization's profits along the lines of the nine dimensions I previously listed in Lesson One:

1. Attract more customers and purchases because of customers wanting to support the social purpose.

   As we explored previously through the RECYCLA Chile example, many customers increase purchases because their own customers will buy more due to their preferences for the social-benefit expansion. Suppliers play a role in increasing that responsiveness by customers' customers through making it possible for RECYCLA Chile to do more complete and responsible recycling than it could accomplish on its own or achieve through alternative suppliers.

2. Obtain premium pricing due to the strength of customer desire to support the social purpose or to the marketing benefits received.

   Because more complete recycling through the most effective suppliers costs RECYCLA Chile more, the company is able to improve its case for charging a premium price by pointing to the advantageous waste treatment that premium prices allow it to afford.

3. Reduce costs by receiving volunteer help or reduced charges from suppliers who favor the purpose for the increased social benefits.

   Not every environmentally conscientious supplier is going to be willing to take less money for performing its work. Yet where the appeal of the social purpose is great enough, some suppliers will charge less. When that happens, the potential of reaching the profit-increase goal is higher.

   If a supplier has an advantaged business model (or can be encouraged to develop or adopt one) that includes extensive use of highly effective volunteers, more social benefits can be provided while the supplier's and your company's profits can be higher.

4. Experience fewer costs due to a higher drive among employees, partners, and suppliers for productivity, willingness to work harder in less favorable conditions, and demanding less in payments and benefits.

Some suppliers will be so serious about providing more social benefits that they will be able to accomplish much more than their competitors, potentially reducing not only what they charge but also what costs your customers incur in addition to the price of your offerings.

5. Avoid investments due to stakeholders doing more of such required investing.

   In the case of RECYCLA Chile, some best practices for recycling require major investments by suppliers. By being able to send partially processed electronic debris to such suppliers, RECYCLA Chile is able to avoid making what would otherwise be much less efficient investments in facilities that it would operate.

6. Increase sensitivity to improving cash flow by all stakeholders because of its effect on providing more for those who receive social benefits.

   Some suppliers will allow more time to pay that enables a new or struggling customer to have more cash on hand. When an inspiring social benefit is at stake, such terms may become more generous than usual.

7. Encourage innovative business models that build on the trust and preference for providing and receiving the social benefits.

   Suppliers who are conscientious about providing the social benefits may well notice and conceive of better ways to accomplish benefit-enhancing tasks. I was struck by this perspective while putting insect poison around the foundation of my house. The company's new packaging design greatly reduces the risk of someone being poisoned or the poison being mishandled after being used. The impressive design was undoubtedly the result of some supplier's fine work.

8. Potentially receive subsidies from various stakeholders to pay for launching, expanding, or sustaining the benefit provision.

   For many social benefits, the costs that society bears can be quite substantial when the benefits aren't adequately provided. By working with local suppliers in many areas, an organization can increase the likelihood of gaining such subsidies from local agencies and governments representing regions where suppliers operate.

9. Directly create more demand for the firm's offerings due to the resulting social benefits.

   Suppliers can play a key role in increasing awareness that a customer is using the best possible practices, such as by providing certifications of the sort that RECYCLA Chile does for its environmentally conscious customers.

In reviewing this list, I'm sure you were struck that the potential to accomplish much more is quite substantial. The thought may have crossed your mind that few suppliers are going to be already doing all such things. I agree with you.

The process of gaining these advantages from suppliers has to begin by explaining to potential suppliers what help you need from them, why that help is important to obtain, and what benefits society and the supplier will gain from making such advantages available to you.

After such a communication, you might discover that the largest and most respected firms won't want to make any changes to accommodate what you want to do ... unless you are an enormous organization. You'll probably find that smaller, newer organizations led by people who feel called to provide more social benefits will be more interested in working with you to accomplish what you have in mind. Although it may be a disadvantage at first to work with such less experienced and less well-endowed suppliers, if you sense that they can ultimately deliver a lot more of what you need, give them a chance.

Be prepared also to participate in helping suppliers appreciate what the ideal business models are for them to use in support of what you want to accomplish. You may also have to provide technical assistance in some cases so that the right results are achieved.

Realize that accomplishing all that you desire may not be possible at first. Work with the potential suppliers to develop a transition process to begin delivering new advantages, then gradually add still more advantages in some logical fashion until all of the advantages are being provided in effective ways.

What's the key lesson? *An organization that sincerely wants to accelerate its profitable growth can be helped by expanding the current level of social benefits by a much larger (more than 20 times) multiple than the profit increases that it gains from providing the social benefits well in ways that are supported by strong contributions from suppliers that the organization's own efforts cannot match.*

Your Lesson Four Assignments

1. Identify how selecting and developing the right suppliers can help increase the quantity and types of social benefits provided in ways that attract many more customers and offering and social-benefit end users, and more visible support from them for your organization's activities.

2. Evaluate how each social-benefit increase from selecting and developing the right suppliers would affect each of the nine categories of potential sales and profit increases listed in this and the prior three lessons in terms of attracting and obtaining more

support from existing and new stakeholders who are not your suppliers.

3. Search other industries to find practices that could be brought into your industry to greatly expand the contribution that suppliers make to the value of your social-benefit increases to current and potential end users for offerings and social benefits.

4. Before making your final supplier selections, test the effectiveness of potential suppliers to help you adjust your offerings and social benefits to be more useful and abundant.

Lesson Five

Energize Employees

Now in the church that was at Antioch
there were certain prophets and teachers:
Barnabas, Simeon who was called Niger,
Lucius of Cyrene, Manaen
who had been brought up with
Herod the tetrarch, and Saul.

As they ministered to the Lord and fasted,
the Holy Spirit said,
"Now separate to Me Barnabas and Saul
for the work to which I have called them."

Then, having fasted and prayed, and
laid hands on them, they sent them *away.*

— Acts 13:1-3 (NKJV)

While many people work to earn a living, Acts 13:1-3 (NKJV) points out that some people are called by God to do certain work that will greatly advance His Kingdom by making good use of the remarkable gifts and talents He has provided. With God's supernatural support to provide fruitful opportunities, such individuals may well accomplish what to nonbelievers would seem like miracles. In terms of an organization that's seeking to solve serious social problems and greatly expand the provision of needed social benefits far beyond the profit the company can hope to gain, having employees who are called to find such solutions and expand such provisions should make all the difference. While many employers seek to have employees who seem the best qualified in secular terms, it would be wiser to see if employees are called by God to accomplish what needs to be done. As your enterprise engages in doing more to advance God's Kingdom, you should expect to find more people who are so called.

In this lesson, our focus shifts into the role of employees in achieving the sixth complementary 2,000 percent solution, expanding social benefits by 20 times more than the profits that are gained. I first discuss how employees can help or hurt providing the nine types of advantages for expanding an organization's profits while increasing the supply of scarce social benefits:

1. Attract more customers and purchases because of customers wanting to support the social purpose.

   It takes more than just asserting that your organization serves a social purpose to succeed in gaining more purchases. Customers have to perceive that this work is being done with conviction and integrity. Employees who act in ways that undermine confidence among current and potential customers can drive away potential interest. Employees who go the extra mile to take the right actions and to assure customers that all is well can, instead, greatly increase interest in and excitement among current and potential customers because of the social purpose being accomplished. More customers and purchases can follow.

2. Obtain premium pricing due to the strength of customer desire to support the social purpose or to the marketing benefits received.

The better job that employees do in serving the social purpose, the more customers will feel justified in paying premium prices for the offerings. If, instead, employees do a lackadaisical job, current and potential customers may feel victimized by the pricing and avoid purchasing.

3. Reduce costs by receiving volunteer help or reduced charges from suppliers who favor the purpose for the increased social benefits.

   Employees are essential to attracting more volunteer help and reduced charges from suppliers. Many employees will feel threatened by volunteers, fearing that their own jobs are in jeopardy. Emotionally secure, mature employees who favor the social purpose welcome the volunteers so that more can be accomplished. In the same way, those employees who want to strongly support the social purpose will be continually looking for more effective suppliers and ways to work with suppliers more efficiently to provide better and more results at less cost.

4. Experience fewer costs due to a higher drive among employees, partners, and suppliers for productivity, willingness to work harder in less favorable conditions, and demanding less in payments and benefits.

   In many organizations, the employee attitude is more likely to be, "Ask not what I can do for the company, but ask what the company can do for me." This attitude will delay or prevent many helpful improvements from being discovered and utilized. I rarely recall visiting a profit-seeking organization where employees were eagerly seeking higher productivity, were thriving from hard work in less favorable conditions, and were happy to accept pay and benefits that were well below comparable organizations because of a desire to help customers and society benefit more. The spiritual commitment among employees at the Aravind Eye Care System seems to be a major exception, at least through the time when the founder was still alive. I have often seen such commitment among Christian nonprofit organizations.

5. Avoid investments due to stakeholders doing more of such required investing.

   In many cases, employees are the ones who need to find ways for stakeholders to do more and to help such stakeholders to understand the rationale and benefits gained from helping out in such ways. Employees, too, can reduce investment by being willing to work in ways that require less investment. You can see such willingness at Aravind Eye Care System. Operating rooms and work schedules were adjusted so that many investments for eye operations could be reduced by more than 80 percent for each procedure.

6. Increase sensitivity to improving cash flow by all stakeholders because of its effect on providing more for those who receive social benefits.

   Cash flow isn't improved by accident. It gets better from upgraded business models developed and implemented by people who take care of the cash resources more carefully than if they were spending their own money ... because they are highly aware of all the good that extra cash can do. Most of such caring concern is spearheaded by employees.

7. Encourage innovative business models that build on the trust and preference for providing and receiving the social benefits.

   Not only does your organization need better business models ... but so do your stakeholders. Your employees are going to be essential to helping others become interested in and capable of making such changes .... and then acting in trustworthy ways so that others are willing to rely on them.

8. Potentially receive subsidies from various stakeholders to pay for launching, expanding, or sustaining the benefit provision.

   Subsidies are most likely paid when they will provide a great harvest of benefits for those who most need help. Employees will be essential to make that case to other stakeholders, sustain belief among other stakeholders in the rightness of providing such subsidies, and be sure the increased benefits are fully supplied.

9. Directly create more demand for the firm's offerings due to the resulting social benefits.

   Here's another place where continuing innovation has great value. When employees deeply care about providing more benefits, they will seek ways to provide benefits that will, in turn, enable more benefits to be provided ... whether by attracting more volunteer activity or by wise focus on what can be done to better apply the organization's resources and those of other stakeholders.

For the optimal employee fit, you as an organizational leader have several challenges:

1. Recruit employees who want to enormously expand the social benefits that your organization provides now, are able to do so, and will work tirelessly to create such results.

2. Develop employees so that their desire increases for enormously expanding the social benefits your organization provides

now, their capabilities to do so, and their willingness to work faithfully to create such results.

3. Encourage employees to attract, inspire, and assist the stakeholders (and any employees those stakeholders have) to do the same.

Naturally, making such changes to meet the challenges is easiest to do if your organizational culture already supports such values and orientations. If your culture doesn't, consider setting up a new, small organization that will focus just on this opportunity.

If you don't have any organization, you face the challenge of building one. If that's the case, you should also consider business models that rely more on highly motivated suppliers. You'll probably find it easier to gain the kind of support you need by coordinating such suppliers with your employees, rather than to create a major organization from scratch filled with people who have the right kinds of commitment, capabilities, and willingness.

In any event, I strongly encourage you to try people before adding them to work in such a role. Put them into a training program first where they can have a chance to work on what you want them to do, to see how it feels, and to find out how good they are at it. Those who successfully emerge will then have powerful insights into how to attract, improve, and encourage future employees.

In making these changes, consider the seventh step in the 2,000 percent solution process. If you don't recall the directions for that step, I encourage you to reread that material now in *The 2,000 Percent Solution* (AMACOM, 1999) and in *The 2,000 Percent Solution Workbook* (iUniverse, 2005). That information should give you helpful insights into how to go about these critical tasks.

I also suspect that many of such employees who have been recruited, developed, and encouraged will have already developed a deep spiritual faith that fills them with a desire to serve others in self-sacrificing ways. While I suggest you not assume that will be the case, certainly keep an eye open for ways that supernatural support can be provided to your enterprise by having such employees who can make your organization more fruitful for God through their faithfulness and prayers.

What's the key lesson? *An organization that sincerely wants to accelerate its profitable growth can be helped by increasing the current level of social benefits by a much larger (more than 20 times) multiple than the profit increases that it gains from providing the social-benefit increases in ways that are supported by strong contributions from employees that the organization's other stakeholders cannot accomplish on their own.*

Your Lesson Five Assignments

1. Identify how selecting, developing, and encouraging employees can help increase the quantity and types of social benefits to attract many more customers and offering and social-benefit end users, and more visible support from them for your organization's activities.

2. Evaluate how each social-benefit increase from selecting, developing, and encouraging employees would affect each of the nine categories of potential sales and profit increases listed in this and the prior four lessons in terms of attracting and obtaining more support from existing and new stakeholders who aren't employees, customers, or end users.

3. Search other industries to find practices that could be brought into your industry to greatly expand the contributions that employees make to the value of your social-benefit increases for current and potential end users of offerings and social benefits.

4. Test the effectiveness of specific employees in adding value to offerings and social benefits before making your final hiring decisions and job assignments.

Lesson Six

Engage Employees' Families

So they called these days Purim, after the name Pur.
Therefore, because of all the words of this letter,
what they had seen concerning this matter,
and what had happened to them,
the Jews established and imposed it upon themselves
and their descendants and all who would join them,
that without fail they should celebrate
these two days every year,
according to the written instructions
and according to the prescribed *time,*
that *these days* should be *remembered and*
kept throughout every generation, every family,
every province, and every city,
that these days of Purim should not fail
to be observed *among the Jews, and*
that *the memory of them should not perish*
among their descendants.

— Esther 9:26-28 (NKJV)

Esther 9:26-28 (NKJV) explains how Queen Esther's courage in opposing Haman to save the Jews came to be remembered thousands of years later. From this example, we are reminded how powerful it can be to appreciate that something good is happening and be inspired to encourage others to learn about the good performance. Similarly, companies can set such a good example for increasing social benefits that employees' families will eagerly tell others, and many listeners will decide to honor the company by either increasing their support or becoming stakeholders.

In this lesson, we discuss positively engaging employees' families, a stakeholder group that most often receives attention in terms of considering ways to avoid doing harm to them. When it comes to increasing social benefits by 400 times and your organization's profits by at least 20 times, there's a more positive opportunity: providing added credibility for the proposition that what your organization is doing has value that deserves wider and more support. While such influence once would have been mostly limited to word of mouth in the neighborhood and community, employees' families can also be important influencers among those who don't live in the same communities because of today's social-media explosion.

Since employees' families aren't going to be on the payroll, the nature and quantity of their efforts and contributions are somewhat harder to predict. I would like, however, to suggest five ways that credibility might be added through these families:

1. Some friends and neighbors who know that an employee works for an organization engaged in some high-profile activity that's supposed to have a large positive effect on many people will be naturally curious to know if the reports are true and to learn more details.

   When employees and their families share encouraging stories and facts about what the company is doing, the information is usually treated much more seriously than if a renowned news organization made a similar report. As a result, such stories and information can easily spread to thousands of people from a single mention by a member of an employee's family.

   The opportunity to gain credibility is quite large because most people realize that large claims made by executives and professionals are usually filled with more hot air than actual results.

2. The opposite potential to influence also exists. Many employees' families complain about the organizations that family members work for to friends and neighbors. The family members may reveal flaws in offerings, poor working conditions, unfair treatment, and moral lapses among those who work for the organization.

   If employees' families are convinced that the social benefits are actually being provided in the way that the public is being told, there is an opportunity for employees' families to see the organization as a positive influence, rather than as a negative one (the way many employers are viewed). When such a perception occurs, employees' families may decide to overlook or not to mention the sorts of bad things that are often revealed to outsiders. When this happens, the organization's reputation may climb closer to where it should be.

3. While many employees' families will not seek volunteer roles, some of them may indirectly encourage others to do so. During casual conversations with friends and neighbors, stories and information about volunteer roles will be shared. If the employee's family speaks positively about the contributions that are being made, some people who are looking for volunteer opportunities will decide to look into what the company's choices are.

4. In many cases, interested employees' families can also help your company to spot mistakes, identify untapped opportunities, and improve understanding of what you are trying to do by reporting instances that are at odds with your intended purposes. Many organizations fail to seek such information and delay learning about major opportunities to improve.

5. Employees' families can also be talent scouts, encouraging highly skilled, motivated people to look for employment at your organization.

Keeping these five potential influences in mind, let's also examine how employees' families might contribute to the nine major ways that serving social purposes often adds to company profits:

1. Attract more customers and purchases because of customers wanting to support the social purpose.

   Positive comments made by employees' families and silence about some negative situations known to the families can certainly help. If your organization provides visible tokens of providing the social benefits, such as coffee mugs and shirts, employees' families may choose to use or wear such items ... adding to the visibility of the company's approach.

2. Obtain premium pricing due to the strength of customer desire to support the social purpose or to the marketing benefits received.

   Credible stories told by employees' families about how premium prices greatly expand the social benefits provided and their value to beneficiaries can be important influences for encouraging customers to purchase at higher prices.

3. Reduce costs by receiving volunteer help or reduced charges from suppliers who favor the purpose for the increased social benefits.

   Word of mouth from employees' families may well help attract more volunteer help. Stories told and comments made by employees' families can improve perceptions in a community, bolstering identification with the purposes of the company's approach that suppliers feel.

4. Experience fewer costs due to a higher drive among employees, partners, and suppliers for productivity, willingness to work harder in less favorable conditions, and demanding less in payments and benefits.

   Employees whose grandparents, parents, aunts, uncles, siblings, spouses, in-laws, and children praise them for contributing to the organization are surely going to be motivated to do more in these dimensions. These employees will certainly not move to another employer unless there's extreme provocation or a large opportunity.

5. Avoid investments due to stakeholders doing more of such required investing.

   If community reputation has been increased enough because of comments by employees' families, some stakeholders may feel encouraged to bear added burdens to help.

6. Increase sensitivity to improving cash flow by all stakeholders because of its effect on providing more for those who receive social benefits.

   When employees' families are delighted because beneficiaries' lives are being transformed by the added benefits, such information will influence employees to want to do more with less so that greater benefits can be provided and the esteem in which they are held by their families will further increase.

7. Encourage innovative business models that build on the trust and preference for providing and receiving the social benefits.

Employees' families can be good sources of ideas for innovative ways to get things done. Realizing the praise that they might earn from their families for such activities will certainly keep employees more focused on trying to find ways to improve. Be sure employees' families are always invited to ceremonies where outstanding employee contributions in this regard are recognized.

8. Potentially receive subsidies from various stakeholders to pay for launching, expanding, or sustaining the benefit provision.

   Employees' families can be active in attending meetings and hearings, and demonstrating support for the company's activities. Such greater visibility can help attract media attention and more positive word-of-mouth comments.

9. Directly create more demand for the firm's offerings due to the resulting social benefits.

   The more pride that a family feels in what the employee is doing with the company, the more the employee and family will want to do to enhance this feeling. As successes follow, a desire for more success will increase for the employee, as well as for the family. This reinforcing sequence helps create ongoing advances similar to the way that a successful college sports program helps ensure future performance by making it easier to attract and retain top student athletes.

As you better appreciate now, engaging employees' families presents opportunities to further encourage employees, to spot ways to improve, to enhance the word-of-mouth reputation of the organization, and to provide more community credibility at essentially no cost through the increasingly important megaphone of social media.

What's the key lesson? *An organization that sincerely wants to accelerate its profitable growth can be helped by increasing the current level of social benefits by a much larger (more than 20 times) multiple than the profit increases that it gains from providing the social-benefit increases in ways that will increase engagement by and support of employees' families.*

Your Lesson Six Assignments

1. Identify how engaging employees' families might help increase the quantity and types of social benefits provided to attract many more customers, offering and social-benefit end users, and more visible support from them for your organization.

2. Identify how engaging employees' families might help increase purchases from customers who will pay premium prices, and provide other economic benefits in support of the social purposes and your organization's ability to profit from expanding benefits.

3. Evaluate how each social-benefit increase from engaging employees' families could affect each of the nine categories of potential sales and profit increases listed in this and the prior five lessons in terms of attracting and obtaining more support from existing and new stakeholders who aren't in employees' families.

4. Search other industries to find practices that could be brought to your industry for greatly expanding the contributions that engaged employees' families make to the value of your social-benefit increases for current and potential customers, and for end users of offerings and social benefits.

5. Look beyond what anyone else has done to engage employees' families in every conceivable way to expand social benefits by at least 400 times and company profits by 20 times or more.

Lesson Seven

Open Up Owners

But as they were loosing the colt,
the owners of it said to them,
"Why are you loosing the colt?"

And they said, "The Lord has need of him."

Then they brought him to Jesus.
And they threw their own clothes on the colt,
and they set Jesus on him.

— Luke 19:33-35 (NKJV)

Luke 19:33-35 (NKJV) describes what happened when Jesus' disciples went to fetch a colt that He had directed them to borrow. Part of His instructions included what to say if anyone challenged their borrowing of the colt. After that, Jesus sat on the colt and made His triumphal entry into Jerusalem on Palm Sunday. Had the disciples not had a good reason for borrowing the colt, they would undoubtedly been considered as being thieves. Instead, the owners appear to have agreed to lend the colt, possibly feeling honored by the request. We should be similarly cautious about assuming owners will want us to engage in increasing social benefits as a means of growing profits. A careful explanation will be needed before some owners will want to support such an activity.

We turn our attention now to making such changes from the owners' perspective. Some might argue that I should have started with them. I think not. Let me explain.

Owners will clearly have to agree with this way of expanding company profits, or it won't be possible to perform. Without approval, hostile owners would simply seek to replace management, and either succeed or create such a battle that little progress could occur.

But before you can hope to persuade an owner that this complementary 2,000 percent solution goal is a good idea, you need to know more about the idea ... and be able to describe some specific ways that it might be accomplished. The last few lessons' assignments should have greatly helped in this regard.

Let's first consider why the nine types of advantages for expanding an organization's profits while greatly increasing the supply of social benefits could appeal to owners in terms of both economic and non-economic advantages. In doing so, I urge you to keep these thoughts in the back of your mind and not presume that they are the case for any given owner.

1. Attract more customers and purchases because of customers wanting to support the social purpose.

   Many wealthy people no sooner make a lot of money than they begin spending it in ways that provide social benefits. Bill Gates, founder of Microsoft, is an influential example. For instance, Warren Buffett, the billionaire investor, has already pledged most of his estate to the Gates Foundation.

   While motives for doing so vary from owner to owner, clearly some owners find it more fun to "do good" than just to "profit themselves." In many cases, their normal business activities don't provide many opportunities to "do good" so they seek new outlets to have such experiences. By combining the two opportunities of doing good and profiting themselves through a business they own some or all of, there are substantial opportunities for gaining personal satisfaction.

Many wealthy people also crave things that simply being rich doesn't provide, such as popularity, public esteem, recognition, and feeling appreciated. If an organization that they own is doing great things through expanding social benefits, there will be many occasions when the owners will be recognized for their "leadership" (even if they aren't in management) roles in helping the community or society.

2. Obtain premium pricing due to the strength of customer desire to support the social purpose or to the marketing benefits received.

More owners would like to be part of a premium-priced business than a discount business. Why? Typically, the premium-priced business earns higher profit margins. There's also more personal prestige because the pricing indicates a strong preference for what the organization does. In many areas of life, such prestige is sought at great expense without much success, such as in breeding and racing horses, owning sports teams, and possessing so-called trophy properties. (In practice, each of these investments may simply be expensive "white elephants" in disguise.)

Many others envy such an owner, which makes the distinction all the sweeter for some.

There's also an element of implied "higher IQ" involved ... and most people would like to be thought of as intelligent ... as well as caring. That's especially true for some of those who aren't very much of either one.

3. Reduce costs by receiving volunteer help or reduced charges from suppliers who favor the purpose for the increased social benefits.

Rich people are used to being overcharged as well as being targeted by others as "easy pigeons." As a result, they often seek seclusion and privacy where access and such vulnerability can be reduced.

The thought of volunteers and other organizations seeking to do their organization favors will be especially refreshing and intriguing to many owners, especially those who normally have been expected to do the most extensive volunteering and providing of favors for others.

4. Experience fewer costs due to a higher drive among employees, partners, and suppliers for productivity, willingness to work harder in less favorable conditions, and demanding less in payments and benefits.

   Similar to the preceding point, owners are more used to there being a wrestling match with employees over gaining benefits from any performance improvements that occur. To be in a circumstance where employees are willing to sacrifice, along with owners, will be a new and refreshing experience, one that will open opportunities to have more friendly and constructive relations with employees.

5. Avoid investments due to stakeholders doing more of such required investing.

   There's an ownership benefit here that extends beyond higher profits. Such an organization will need to borrow less money and to sell less equity. When capital needs are so reduced, higher dividends, more share repurchases, and higher stock-price value occur ... all mainstream advantages that any owner would like to increase.

6. Increase sensitivity to improving cash flow by all stakeholders because of its effect on providing more for those who receive social benefits.

   Once again, such a focus translates into greater stock value. You can see the owners' broad smiles from far away.

7. Encourage innovative business models that build on the trust and preference for providing and receiving the social benefits.

   This is the most important form of improved innovation that any organization can provide to an owner in terms of increasing long-term value of shares and reducing the risk of loss.

8. Potentially receive subsidies from various stakeholders to pay for launching, expanding, or sustaining the benefit provision.

   Wealthy people are used to being taxed more heavily and discriminated against by governments, except when they make hefty campaign contributions. To receive substantial funding from governments and others will be especially sweet to owners who bear a sense of being abused in these regards.

9. Directly create more demand for the firm's offerings due to the resulting social benefits.

   This is another great way to further expand stock value and to reduce future risk of loss in that value.

Although these potential advantages are very substantial and can greatly appeal to owners, realize that if you aren't the majority owner of the organization, the other owners may not see it the same way you do. Timing and credibility are important to gaining owners' support. I suggest that you first focus on establishing that your way of increasing social benefits by at least 400 times while increasing profits by 20 times is working well on a small scale before seeking to apply the solution throughout the organization's activities.

Alternatively, consider setting up a new enterprise for just these activities that will have a different set of owners from the existing organization. Arrange for the financial relationships between the two organizations to take full advantage of any successes each one makes so that all stakeholders and owners will be pleased when one or the other makes an advance. Danone did just that by joint venturing with the Grameen Bank in Bangladesh to provide yogurt-based products to poor children, while providing more income opportunities for poor farmers and women distributors.

In any case, before taking any steps sound out owners about their current attitudes and what evidence they would want to see before they would fully support this sixth complementary 2,000 percent solution.

In some cases, you may be pleasantly surprised to find unexpected allies and opportunities. Many wealthy people pal around with one another and have contacts that can be very helpful for opening doors needed to add many more social benefits through joining with partners and supporters you would have a hard time attracting on your own.

Rather than trying to "teach" this lesson to owners, be prepared to "learn" it at their knees. In some cases, owners may even be willing to make needed changes that can accelerate progress beyond the improvements that could be made without their support.

What's the key lesson? *An organization that sincerely wants to accelerate its profitable growth can be helped by increasing the current level of social benefits by a much larger (more than 20 times) multiple than the profit increases that it gains from providing the social-benefit increases in ways that are supported by the owners' personal and financial self-interests.*

Your Lesson Seven Assignments

1. Identify how owners' support might help increase the quantity and types of social benefits to attract many more customers and offering and social-benefit end users, and more visible support from them for your organization's activities.

2. Evaluate how each social-benefit increase from carefully developing support from owners could affect each of the nine categories of potential sales and profit increases listed in this and the prior six lessons in terms of attracting and increasing support from existing and new stakeholders who aren't owners.

3. Search other industries to find practices that could be brought into your industry to greatly expand the contribution that owners make to the value of your social-benefit increases to current and potential customers, and end users for offerings and social benefits.

4. Test and prove the effectiveness of programs on a small scale before asking owners to make any investments or personal sacrifices to support new directions.

Lesson Eight

Add Dream-Team Partners

Then He got into one of the boats, which was Simon's,
and asked him to put out a little from the land.

And He sat down and taught the multitudes from the boat.

When He had stopped speaking, He said to Simon,
"Launch out into the deep and let down your nets for a catch."

But Simon answered and said to Him,
"Master, we have toiled all night and caught nothing;
nevertheless at Your word I will let down the net."

And when they had done this,
they caught a great number of fish, and
their net was breaking.

So they signaled to their *partners*
in the other boat to come and help them.

And they came and filled both the boats,
so that they began to sink.

When Simon Peter saw it,
he fell down at Jesus' knees, saying,
"Depart from me, for I am a sinful man, O Lord!"

For he and all who were with him were astonished
at the catch of fish which they had taken;
and so also were *James and John,*
the sons of Zebedee,
who were partners with Simon.

And Jesus said to Simon,
"Do not be afraid. From now on you will catch men."

So when they had brought their boats to land,
they forsook all and followed Him.

— Luke 5:3-11 (NKJV)

In Luke 5:3-11 (NKJV), Jesus first finds a willing volunteer in Simon who lends his boat and labor to help Him address the multitude. After providing this service, Jesus provides a bountiful catch of fish, one so substantial that it swamps Simon's boat as well as the boat of his partners James and John. Properly realizing the supernatural source of what had just occurred, Simon and his partners were filled with faith that caused them to abandon their fishing businesses to follow Jesus, ultimately becoming some of His most important and dependable disciples. In so doing, four men formed a new partnership with Jesus that eventually led to expanding God's Kingdom. Notice in this example that while the fishermen had no experience in preaching or attracting believers, Jesus provided what was needed through His example, teaching, and dispatch of the Holy Spirit. Similarly, you should seek the highest potential in your partners, potential that will lead to accomplishing more in expanding social benefits while earning greater profits.

In this lesson, we consider adding dream-team partners to make a more successful shift into providing 400 times more social benefits and earning 20 times more profits. Let me begin by explaining what I mean by dream-team partners.

When professional basketball players were first allowed to play in the Olympic Games, the very best professional players in the United States were eager to compete. The resulting squad was nicknamed the "Dream Team" because no one could think of any outstanding player who wasn't on it. That team was undefeated, usually winning by large margins.

Having a social purpose to increase benefits by 400 times is a powerful lure to attract potential partners who either care about that purpose or who are excited about the challenge of accomplishing it. From having worked with, studied, and written about outstanding executives for many years, I'm always pleased to see how often they tire of merely growing sales, profits, cash flow, and shareholder value, causing them to also look for ways to provide major improvements in social benefits.

While it's often hidden to outsiders, most for-profit enterprises do quite a lot more in the public interest than what's mandated. Some companies follow environmental guidelines that are more stringent than what is legally required. Others seek to hire more handicapped and disadvantaged workers than the minimum spelled out in union agreements and by law. Almost all companies earmark funds or offerings for donations to worthy groups of all kinds, in addition to having foundations that also dispense funds for charitable purposes. Employees are often asked to volunteer unpaid time for all kinds of worthy causes. Some nonprofit organizations are also allowed to make fund-raising pitches at the company's place of business. I'm sure that you know examples of going beyond what's required, perhaps even from your own business.

When an organization also has an opportunity to be a partner in such a search for adding social benefits, there's an extra sense of appropriateness ... especially given that the partnership may well deliver some profits to help justify what is being done. Think of the profit potential as providing camouflage for some hearts that want to give more.

My point is this: If you approach an ideal partner to help you and your organization expand social benefits by 400 times while your partnership benefits from a 20-times profit increase, you will probably succeed in obtaining the assistance that you need. Because whatever initial contribution you need will be relatively easier for an organization that is much larger than yours to bear, I believe such a result is especially likely with such partners.

Part of the reason for my optimism is that organizations are more willing to participate in activities in which they are to be partners than simply suppliers or donors. Why is that? In addition to the potential profit that partners may gain, partners have a greater claim than do suppliers and donors to bragging rights for any results that occur. In addition, accounting rules often permit for-profit companies to charge any losses in minority partnership positions to their balance sheets rather than the profit-and-loss statement. Consequently, generous support may be provided without anyone in a partner's management team receiving any less compensation or owners having any reason to complain that their profits have been reduced.

In some instances, such partners may also see some additional economic advantages, such as developing a technology that they can use for other purposes, gaining favorable publicity that will add to sales and profits, attracting and retaining people with valuable skills, and enhancing work satisfaction for decision makers.

As a result, think very carefully about what kinds and degrees of benefits can be provided to one potential partner versus another. From understanding this perspective, you'll have a better idea of what you can ask a potential partner to do and still obtain a reasonable result for the efforts involved. Let's look at this issue in terms of the nine potential benefit dimensions that we have been studying for the impact on the potential partner:

1. Attract more customers and purchases because of customers wanting to support the social purpose.

There are three classes of potential partners that will be especially attracted:

(a) Those organizations that have a bad reputation now for harming society in ways related to what the social benefits seek to offset
(b) Those organizations that have the best reputation now for helping society in related ways
(c) Those organizations whose customers and end users are most sensitive to wanting more of the social benefit to be provided that you are focusing on

In selecting a potential partner to ask first, I encourage you to consider both the likelihood that an organization will want to actively participate and how great its potential contributions could be. It's a mistake to emphasize just one or the other quality, because it does no good to be working with the most talented organization if you have no access to that organization's best people. Also, it does little good to have an enthusiastic partner that can add few benefits.

In terms of this factor, I think that Grameen Bank's recruitment of Danone as its partner can serve as a good example for our discussion purposes. While many food manufacturers could certainly help provide new nutritional products at lower costs, Danone's identity is so closely identified with yogurt that it would gain more potential benefits from the positive publicity that could emerge from such a partnership than would most dairy food manufacturers, and far more benefit than those organizations that sell harmful foods and consumer products. This initially was also a partnership that would most help Muslims, a religious group with which a French company probably doesn't have an optimal image and reputation.

2. Obtain premium pricing due to the strength of customer desire to support the social purpose or to the marketing benefits received.

   For a large partner, the scale and popularity of the social benefits provided would have to be quite substantial before public perceptions would be increased enough to support more premium pricing. In the Danone case, the Bangladesh partnership is a quite small one. It would have to be expanded by many hundreds of times in Bangladesh and be taken to many more countries before Danone might see a reputational impact on pricing for its dairy products.

3. Reduce costs by receiving volunteer help or reduced charges from suppliers who favor the purpose for the increased social benefits.

   Such benefits are much more likely to occur if the partnership is the beginning of what will become a major, ongoing joint activity with profits being earned by the partner.

   In the Danone case, the partnership was more akin to a research-and-development joint venture with Danone providing the technology and Grameen Bank bringing the consumer and sociological knowledge to define a low-cost business model.

   It's clear, however, that Danone could choose to adopt some aspects of the joint-venture model to its activities in other developing nations by engaging more local farmers, poor women as distributors, and rural people to work in food production. If that direction were taken by Danone with its existing products, Danone would gain important cost advantages.

4. Experience fewer costs due to a higher drive among employees, partners, and suppliers for productivity, willingness to work harder in less favorable conditions, and demanding less in payments and benefits.

Such cost benefits are most likely to occur due to the potential partner's own activities, as it directs work by highly motivated, talented employees with access to proprietary knowledge and technology. Such an organization might see this kind of partnership as a launching pad for developing new kinds of businesses that it could not do on its own that would have a much lower cost base due to insights learned from the joint venture.

Danone's technical inputs provided exactly such benefits to the joint venture. Some of those gains might also apply to Danone's existing operations.

5. Avoid investments due to stakeholders doing more of such required investing.

Again, your potential partner is probably more likely to be a source of such investment capital rather than someone who benefits from it, especially if you are seeking technical support and development assistance. If part of the eventual success relies on reducing investments to make the offerings or to provide benefits, then a partner might well gain in traditional activities or from a vastly expanded joint venture that succeeded in improving this dimension of its business model.

6. Increase sensitivity to improving cash flow by all stakeholders because of its effect on providing more for those who receive social benefits.

Such development-stage partnerships usually have little money to invest. Keeping cash costs down is essential for maintaining a venture until such time as it can financially sustain itself. Either your partner will have so many funds that this factor won't matter in the development stage or the overall cost will be quite low.

7. Encourage innovative business models that build on the trust and preference for providing and receiving the social benefits.

   I believe that it is in this dimension that most partners can hope to gain the most practical, as opposed to emotional, advantages from their participation. By having nontraditional partners, new kinds of stakeholders and different working relationships will be forged that can provide substantial, ongoing advantages to any partner that does a good job of nurturing these relationships.

8. Potentially receive subsidies from various stakeholders to pay for launching, expanding, or sustaining the benefit provision.

   When the activity takes place outside of the partner's home country, such subsidies are much more likely due to your participation. Your relationship could be helpful for opening doors for the partner to other kinds of activities in your nation with access to other subsidies.

9. Directly create more demand for the firm's offerings due to the resulting social benefits.

   This benefit, if present, will make it easier for a potential partner to participate by realizing that major future commitments of funds, resources, and time are likely to be modest ... or profitable. Danone, for instance, sought a business model that would be self-sustaining through stakeholders becoming owners, except for occasional needs to develop new products in related food areas.

   Whether Danone would have looked at the opportunity in this way if it perceived the potential to build a profitable large business is an unanswered question. The initial idea was so loosely structured that there was no reason to think that a major enterprise would emerge.

Although a few of these potential advantages are substantial enough to greatly appeal to partners, realize that the emotional appeal of using God-given talents for highly beneficial social purposes is always going to be a major part of the appeal to any partner. Once general interest is established, looking at these practical advantages will have a large influence on how much time, money, effort, and talent your potential partner will be willing to commit.

In assessing potential partners, be careful not to be taken in by lip service. Look for a track record of being a good partner, especially when problems occur.

Be open to your potential partner suggesting that other partners be added. Take the time to understand the thinking so you'll appreciate what the potential advantages and disadvantages are. In the process, be sure that you don't lose control over what you need to accomplish. If you see the possibility of losing control, consider setting up more than one partnership so that you'll be the majority owner of the entity that will be most important for ongoing success.

What's the key lesson? *An organization that sincerely wants to accelerate its profitable growth can be helped by increasing the current level of social benefits by a much larger (more than 20 times) multiple than the profit increases that it gains from providing the social-benefit increases in ways that are supported by highly talented, motivated partners who have much to gain from succeeding and whose skills add dimensions that you cannot accomplish on your own or with the usual suppliers.*

Your Lesson Eight Assignments

1. Identify how partners' support might help increase the quantity and types of social benefits to attract many more customers and offering and social-benefit end users, and more visible support from them for your organization's activities.

2. Evaluate how each social-benefit increase from carefully developing support from the most useful partners could affect each of the nine categories of potential sales and profit increases listed in this and the prior seven lessons in terms of attracting and obtaining more support from existing and new stakeholders who aren't partners.

3. Search other industries to find practices that could be brought into your industry to greatly expand the contribution that partners make to the value of your social-benefit increases to customers and current and potential end users for offerings and social benefits.

Lesson Nine

Add Different Kinds of Distributors

Nor was there anyone among them who lacked;
for all who were possessors of lands or houses sold them,
and brought the proceeds of the things that were sold,
and laid them *at the apostles' feet; and*
they distributed to each as anyone had need.

— Acts 4:34-35 (NKJV)

After Jesus ascended to Heaven and the Holy Spirit descended on Pentecost, believers lingered in Jerusalem, some of whom were far from home and lacked resources to meet their own needs. As the apostles testified to the resurrection of Jesus, the numbers of believers rapidly grew. All those who had means were moved to sell lands and houses to provide for the needs of brothers and sisters in Christ, trusting the apostles to be faithful distributors of such resources, which they were. Similarly, having trustworthy, Godly distributors of offerings and social benefits can multiply the effective provision of such benefits and profits from doing so.

This lesson focuses on just how adding different kinds of distributors will increase the social benefits you can provide and the profits you can earn. If your business hasn't previously worked with distributors, then please apply this lesson to adding distributors for the first time.

I raise this issue because all the organizations I've studied that expanded social benefits far beyond the percentage of their profit increases found that adding new types of distributors and outreaches was essential to success.

As an example, let's return to the Grameen Bank-Danone joint venture that provides more nutritious yogurt snacks to youngsters in rural Bangladesh. Most of the potential customers for this product are located well away from traditional food stores. In addition, the families of these youngsters don't have refrigeration to keep the snacks fresh. Consequently, these products need to be transported quickly under cool conditions to youngsters who will consume the snacks that day.

If the joint venture had tried to accomplish such distribution with yogurt trucks or some similar distribution method of its own to reach each customer, the costs would have been prohibitively high. What could the joint venture do, instead?

Grameen-Danone recruited mothers in low-income rural families to become distributors. These mothers knew other women who would be interested in the products and could distribute a small daily supply in their local neighborhoods. Yes, trucks were needed, but only to drop off the snacks to these women, much as newspaper publishers make street-corner drops to the newsboys in suburban American neighborhoods who take the papers to each house.

That's enough about someone else's business. Let's focus on your business now in terms of the nine categories for potentially providing many more social benefits and increasing your profits:

1. Attract more customers and purchases because of customers wanting to support the social purpose.

   If the distributors are known to the potential customers, such connections can make it easier to explain and demonstrate the social benefits involved. If the distributors are also customers, that fact can add credibility.

As an example, Aravind Eye Care System encourages its surgical patients to bring other patients to its outreach clinics for free eye screenings. Although the patients receive no pay for this activity, the effect is very much like adding a distribution network comprised of satisfied customers.

If the potential customers are those who don't need the social benefits, but who could gain by using the offering, having distributors who are social beneficiaries can make even more sense for adding interest in and credibility concerning the purchase and use of the offering.

2. Obtain premium pricing due to the strength of customer desire to support the social purpose or to the marketing benefits received.

   Premium pricing will occur much more often where the customer gains profits or substantial personal benefits from the offering, rather than where the customer or end user is a social beneficiary. A weakness in many business models for social enterprises is that they (unlike RECYCLA Chile and Aravind Eye Care System) directly provide products and services only to the poorest people. A better model is to also have a set of offerings for those who can afford to pay a premium for what is provided, and are willing to do so due to a desire to support the social purpose. Distributors who can make the offerings available to this group of highly profitable customers will be important to accomplishing the profit-improvement aspects of this business model.

3. Reduce costs by receiving volunteer help or reduced charges from suppliers who favor the purpose for the increased social benefits.

Clearly, such advantages occur in the business models for the Grameen-Danone joint venture by involving those who distribute the products and in the Aravind Eye Care System by those who attract patients for eye screenings. Your business can similarly benefit by engaging those who need social and offering benefits for distribution roles ... or similar activities.

4. Experience fewer costs due to a higher drive among employees, partners, and suppliers for productivity, willingness to work harder in less favorable conditions, and demanding less in payments and benefits.

   Before beginning to ask former patients to bring family members and friends to free eye-screening clinics, Aravind surgeons and doctors held rural fairs in hopes of attracting potential patients for surgeries conducted at the organization's centralized facilities. Replacing this recruitment and service method with rural outreach clinics staffed by inexpensive technicians serving the people brought by former patients for eye screenings is a much lower-cost way to operate.

   Similarly, women who distribute the Grameen-Danone snacks receive very little pay and work very hard to sell and deliver these products. It would not have been possible to distribute as inexpensively in any other way.

   If you can find social beneficiaries who need work and extra income, chances are that you can engage them in performing some of the distribution activities. Additionally, see if customers and end users are willing to play distribution and distribution-like roles.

5. Avoid investments due to stakeholders doing more of such required investing.

   If distributors are well capitalized, there's certainly potential to eliminate some investments. If the business model itself requires less investment (such as with Grameen-Danone), there's still an overall investment reduction even if the distributors aren't well capitalized. Think of such a contribution as being like "sweat equity."

6. Increase sensitivity to improving cash flow by all stakeholders because of its effect on providing more for those who receive social benefits.

   The former Aravind patients and Grameen-Danone distributors are eager to help. They don't make demands that will harm the organization's cash flow. However, the Grameen-Danone distributors need to be paid very promptly so that they can afford to engage in this activity.

   If higher-profit customers are also to be served, there can be opportunities to receive some extra improvements in cash flow by encouraging such customers to pay more promptly or in advance.

7. Encourage innovative business models that build on the trust and preference for providing and receiving the social benefits.

   This opportunity is the main advantage of adding different kinds of distributors. As a result, it becomes possible to reach more customers, provide more social benefits, and be more credible. In addition, the offerings become much more visible at modest added cost (usually a reduction in cost from any other alternative). In thinking through the alternatives, see how many different kinds of distributors you can add who will deliver substantial social benefits through serving significant amounts of profitable customers.

8. Potentially receive subsidies from various stakeholders to pay for launching, expanding, or sustaining the benefit provision.

If the distributors are social beneficiaries, obtaining subsidies is a definite possibility.

9. Directly create more demand for the firm's offerings due to the resulting social benefits.

   In those cases where the distributors are social beneficiaries or provide access to high-income customers who will want to subsidize the activities for either profit-related or personal reasons, there will be this type of virtuous cycle.

As you can see from this discussion, adding different kinds of distributors opens up many possibilities. I believe that the social enterprises I've studied stopped short in their considerations of what types of distributors to add. These organizations were satisfied to find just one better way. But there may well have been 47 other better ways that they ignored in the process, especially to reach classes of customers and end users who would be highly supportive of the activity and can afford to provide profit- and cash flow-related benefits to their enterprises. I address what you should focus on in the assignments to do better in this regard.

What's the key lesson? *An organization that sincerely wants to accelerate its profitable growth can be helped by increasing the current level of social benefits by a much larger (more than 20 times) multiple than the profit increases that it gains from providing the social-benefit increases in ways that are supported by adding different kinds of distributors who can receive social benefits themselves, increase access to those who need social benefits, and serve sympathetic customers and end users who will support these purposes with purchases at premium prices and by providing cash-flow advantages.*

Your Lesson Nine Assignments

1. Identify how different kinds of distributors (including involving customers and social beneficiaries) might help increase the quantity and types of social benefits provided to attract many more customers and offering and social-benefit end users, and more visible support from them for your organization.

2. Identify how different kinds of distributors (including involving customers and social beneficiaries) might help increase purchases from customers who will pay premium prices and provide other economic benefits in support of the social purposes and your organization's ability to profit from this benefit expansion.

3. Evaluate how each social-benefit increase from carefully developing support from the most helpful of different kinds of distributors could affect each of the nine categories of potential sales and profit increases listed in this and the prior eight lessons in terms of attracting and obtaining more support from existing and new stakeholders who aren't distributors.

4. Search other industries to find practices that could be brought into your industry to greatly expand the contribution that new kinds of distributors make to the value of your social-benefit increases to customers and current and potential end users of offerings and social benefits.

Lesson Ten

Add Volunteers

"Give to him who asks you, and
from him who wants to borrow from you
do not turn away."

— Matthew 5:42 (NKJV)

In the Beatitudes, Jesus presented life principles and directions for building spiritual goodness. For example, we are to do good things for those who do wrong to us. In this context, we can see that the directions in Matthew 5:42 (NKJV) are designed to put love of others ahead of our attachment to material goods and our own ease. In doing so, we also set a good example that will encourage others to do the same. Similarly, when your organization develops a way to greatly expand social benefits, you will bless many people by providing ways for them to selflessly serve as volunteers. In doing so, you'll be helping to expand more dimensions of God's Kingdom than with many of the other lessons in this book.

This lesson looks closely at beneficially adding volunteers. If you already involve volunteers, then consider adding new types. If you don't yet engage any volunteers, you definitely should do so. Hopefully, this lesson will help you to appreciate why their efforts should be an important part of a business model that seeks to expand social benefits by at least 400 times and profits by 20 or more times.

What is a volunteer? Dictionary.com supplies this definition that captures what I intend to describe: "*a person who performs a service willingly and without pay.*" As you can guess, the "willingly" part is to differentiate a volunteer from a slave.

When it comes to nonprofit organizations, many people are accustomed to seeing volunteers buzzing around an office doing some of the clerical duties under the supervision of a small paid staff. In addition, individuals volunteer time to solicit funds from family, friends, and neighbors.

The scope of what can be done in a for-profit enterprise is not fully informed by such experiences. Let's start by considering "interns." The word originally described a "prisoner of war." Since then, it has come to also mean someone in training as part of an educational process. The older word for this relationship is "apprentice." While traditionally interns were paid something (usually a pittance) for their work, in today's difficult economic environment young people who need to gain experience to eventually qualify for a paying job will often work for free in "intern" positions that are little different from what the paid staff is doing. Unless there are laws or union regulations that prohibit doing so, the majority of the work in an enterprise might be done by unpaid interns.

Internships usually come in two types:

1. Those sponsored by an educational institution from which academic credit will be received for the work done
2. Unsponsored internships

In the former case, paperwork may be required for the student to obtain academic credit. In the latter case, there is likely to be a need for writing letters of recommendation that help with future job searches. In addition, interns will need to be covered by some forms of company insurance (such as for accidents on the job). Consequently, interns aren't free, but they are certainly closer to costing the same as volunteers than they are to costing as much as full-time employees do.

Volunteers can also be engaged to obtain customers. Many restaurant chains will provide a donation that's equal to a percentage of any sales received from members of a church, club, or scout group during certain hours on a given day. In doing so, the chains engage members of the organization as volunteers to promote the chain's sales.

Volunteers can also be suppliers, performing services that might otherwise have to be purchased. In some cases, this role might also involve making needed items.

In fact, volunteers can replace virtually any paid stakeholder role. The limits are only found in the imaginations and leadership skills of the business's people.

Keeping that point about using imagination in mind, let's now consider what the potential is for adding volunteers to gain advantages in the nine categories where providing more social benefits can greatly increase company profits, as well:

1. Attract more customers and purchases because of customers wanting to support the social purpose.

   Those who are dedicated to expanding the availability of the social benefits are quite likely to be willing to volunteer for adding customers and purchases that increase the benefits' availability, as the restaurant-chain example shows. When what is gained is more valuable than just receiving a percentage of the amount spent as a donation, the desirability of the benefit should be more effective in attracting and retaining volunteers. Where the social benefits are substantial and sufficiently appealing, it may be possible to form alliances with nonprofit organizations that are already filled with eager volunteers who can be engaged in such activities.

2. Obtain premium pricing due to the strength of customer desire to support the social purpose or to the marketing benefits received.

   Girl Scouts have long sold cookies as a way to raise money for their activities. Almost all of the cookies are purchased by current and former Girl-Scout families. The cookies are not high priced, but they do cost more than the lowest-priced private-label alternatives. Making a Girl Scout smile is often part of the reward that purchasers receive. If you can engage appealing volunteers in your sales activities, you may also receive a premium price.

3. Reduce costs by receiving volunteer help or reduced charges from suppliers who favor the purpose for the increased social benefits.

   If you select (or help develop) suppliers whose business models heavily rely on volunteers, you should also experience lower costs for whatever goods and services they supply to you. Many types of disadvantaged people lack opportunities to work, and your provision of training and contracts for the supplier can open such doors for adding social benefits while reducing costs. People who are not very mobile and want to work from home, but lack Internet connections, are often the most in need of such opportunities.

4. Experience fewer costs due to a higher drive among employees, partners, and suppliers for productivity, willingness to work harder in less favorable conditions, and demanding less in payments and benefits.

   Someone I knew once worked on a movie that was shot by a major producer. My acquaintance was expected to work 12 to 16 hours a day, at least five days a week. While holding a paid position, this person was also supported by all the unsuccessful candidates for her job who took unpaid internships that entailed working these long hours. While the attraction for the interns was the "glamour" of being in the movie business, working on something socially desirable for someone so motivated can be equally or more engaging.

5. Avoid investments due to stakeholders doing more of such required investing.

   Where there are socially beneficial results, organizations that and individuals who support the purpose with volunteer efforts may be willing to loan or share their resources where the increased benefit is sufficiently substantial. In some cases, willingness to do so may be increased by creating a nonprofit organization that can accept donations in exchange for providing tax deductions in those countries (such as the United States) where such economic incentives are also available.

6. Increase sensitivity to improving cash flow by all stakeholders because of its effect on providing more for those who receive social benefits.

   Those who are volunteering are seldom going to be very demanding about being reimbursed for expenses and will usually be very leery of spending more than is required. As long as you keep your promises about what is provided and when, you may get some relief from cash drains especially if volunteers can use their own homes, computers, Internet connections, vehicles, and other "fixed-cost" resources to assist you.

7. Encourage innovative business models that build on the trust and preference for providing and receiving the social benefits.

Many for-profit organizations have gained huge advantages from volunteers who wanted to gain a reputation from their activities (such as Amazon.com reviewers of books and other offerings). Others have been enormously benefited by volunteers who provided free ideas as part of competitions to find the best solutions (especially in global online contests). Nonprofit organizations are always benefiting from volunteers who support the social purposes in almost every possible way. Both for-profit and nonprofit organizations have benefited by training people to gain skills that later provided such volunteers with income opportunities. Nonprofit organizations also attract donors into volunteering by telling others where they work about the volunteering they do and by directly providing some of the social benefits to those in need (such as by writing encouraging letters to sponsored needy children).

I believe that the time is right to combine more of these reasons to volunteer on behalf of organizations as part of the same business model. Additionally, I'm sure that there are other reasons to engage, such as receiving some of the social benefits directly through being a volunteer.

I invite you to let your imagination roam and to engage in whatever experiments you need to test your ideas.

8. Potentially receive subsidies from various stakeholders to pay for launching, expanding, or sustaining the benefit provision.

If the volunteers are able to gain some advantages that are important to them, there's no reason why they won't subsidize the operation. This might be done, for instance, by offering discounts for them to provide more of the social benefits to individuals and groups they especially want to help.

9. Directly create more demand for the firm's offerings due to the resulting social benefits.

In those cases where the volunteers are greatly helped by the social benefits, the potential for no- or low-cost expansion is enormous.

As you can now better appreciate, adding volunteers to play as many stakeholder roles as possible opens up mind-boggling possibilities. I believe that the social enterprises I've studied didn't begin to do enough to see how volunteers could be engaged in many more helpful roles. These enterprises stopped just as soon as they found one way that added more social benefits. But there may well have been many better ways that they ignored in the process.

What's the key lesson from this week's topic? *An organization that sincerely wants to accelerate its profitable growth can be helped by increasing the current level of social benefits by a much larger (more than 20 times) multiple than the profit increases that it gains from providing the social-benefit increases in ways that are supported by adding volunteers who perform many different stakeholder roles.*

Your Lesson Ten Assignments

1. Identify how adding different kinds of volunteers to replace traditional stakeholders might help increase the quantity and types of social benefits provided to attract many more customers and offering and social-benefit end users, and more visible support from them for your organization's activities.

2. Identify how adding different kinds of volunteers might help increase purchases from customers who will pay premium prices and provide other economic benefits in support of these social purposes and your organization's ability to profit from this benefit expansion.

3. Evaluate how each social-benefit increase from carefully developing support from the most helpful of different kinds of volun-

teers could affect each of the nine categories of potential sales and profit increases listed in this and the prior nine lessons in terms of attracting and obtaining more support from existing and new stakeholders who aren't volunteers.

4. Search other industries to find practices that could be brought into your industry to greatly expand the contribution that new kinds of volunteers make to the value of your social-benefit increases to current and potential customers and end users for offerings and social benefits.

5. Look beyond what anyone else has done before to attract and beneficially engage enormous numbers of volunteers in every conceivable role that will expand social benefits by at least 400 times and company profits by 20 times or more.

Lesson Eleven

Raise Awareness and Gain Information with the Help of Interested Strangers

Now, therefore, you are no longer strangers and foreigners,
but fellow citizens with the
saints and members of the household of God,
having been built on the foundation of
the apostles and prophets,
*Jesus Christ Himself being the chief corner*stone,
in whom the whole building, being fitted together,
grows into a holy temple in the Lord,
in whom you also are being built together
for a dwelling place of God in the Spirit.

— Ephesians 2:19-22 (NKJV)

It's easy to see those you don't know yet, those we usually call "strangers," as unimportant, having no effect on us, our plans, or our activities. Yet such individuals may be the missing resources needed to expand social benefits by more than 400 times and profits by 20 times. Ephesians 2:19-22 (NKJV) reminds us that fellow believers are also fellow citizens in God's Kingdom, are children of God, and house the Holy Spirit. We should keep that perspective in mind when considering who else should become involved in and how with the sixth complementary 2,000 percent solution (increasing social benefits by 400 times while profit expands by at least 20 times).

In this lesson, we focus on adding assistance from strangers. You may recall that other 2,000 percent solutions for greatly increasing stakeholder benefits have identified a role for strangers to provide information either as experts or as participants in global online contests to solve difficult challenges.

In the context of this particular 2,000 percent solution, I believe that strangers can also play useful roles in developing information that isn't currently being gathered.

Some of the greatest limitations for expanding social benefits are related to too little being known in many cases about what social benefits are now being received, where the greatest unmet needs are, and what innovative methods can be easily combined and employed that have succeeded in similar circumstances. Yet, those information gaps can be closed by engaging the right strangers. Individual strangers certainly know a great deal about their own situations, as well as those of the people they can easily observe.

Many of such knowledgeable strangers haven't developed any attachment to your purpose. Consequently, they won't initially be interested in becoming volunteers or joining any other formal class of longer-term stakeholders. These strangers may, however, be enticed out of curiosity into performing some valuable, one-time tasks.

For example, you might decide to develop a sample of what's occurring with the provision of current social benefits to those with such needs. Strangers might play a role in finding people to provide the information, or by providing it themselves.

Keeping these roles in mind, let's now consider what the potential is for focusing on adding strangers to gain advantages in the nine categories where providing more social benefits can greatly increase company profits, as well:

1. Attract more customers and purchases because of customers wanting to support the social purpose.

   Strangers are obviously a huge portion of social-media participants. If you make what you want to do appealing enough, you might attract millions of strangers to comment on what you are doing and to share their comments with others whom they know or influence. Some of those contacted are going to become customers or increase their purchases. If the numbers are large enough, the impact can be enormous.

   Through global online contests, strangers can also play a substantial role in identifying and improving ways to attract more customers and purchases.

2. Obtain premium pricing due to the strength of customer desire to support the social purpose or to the marketing benefits received.

   Strangers can participate through social media by testifying about the value of what your organization does in providing social benefits. With enough support, you might attract millions of strangers to comment on what you are doing and to share their comments with tens or hundreds of millions of others whom they know or influence. Some of those contacted are going to be moved to pay premium prices for your offerings to assist in providing increased social benefits.

   Through global online contests, strangers can also play a decisive role in identifying, improving, and combining ways to attract more customers and purchases at premium prices.

3. Reduce costs by receiving volunteer help or reduced charges from suppliers who favor the purpose for the increased social benefits.

Strangers could help you identify volunteers and suppliers who could provide more effective support at lower costs ... or a great many more customer or social benefits at the same cost.

Online contests could again help identify ways to reduce costs by attracting more helpful volunteers and suppliers.

4. Experience fewer costs due to a higher drive among employees, partners, and suppliers for productivity, willingness to work harder in less favorable conditions, and demanding less in payments and benefits.

   Through social-media posts, strangers can help alert potential employees who will display these characteristics in addressing the opportunities your organization offers. As the potential talent pool increases, the effectiveness of what you do should, too.

   Online contests could explore better ways to recruit, encourage, empower, and support such employees.

5. Avoid investments due to stakeholders doing more of such required investing.

   As your organization's social-media presence increases, the prestige of being a stakeholder will greatly expand. When that happens, some of the stakeholders will be able to afford and will want to play bigger roles in providing some of the required investments.

   Online contests can also help identify ways to attract more of such stakeholders who are willing to make these investments on behalf of your organization to serve the social purposes involved.

6. Increase sensitivity to improving cash flow by all stakeholders because of its effect on providing more for those who receive social benefits.

   Stories that you share should help ignite curiosity and support for your enterprise and providing more of the social benefits. Tell the story of cash flow's importance through these anecdotes, and you will affect stakeholder behavior in the right ways.

   Online contests can focus on identifying major ways to enhance cash flow that are not yet being applied.

7. Encourage innovative business models that build on the trust and preference for providing and receiving the social benefits.

   This activity is a natural for greatly benefiting from online contests. Social-media buzz could help increase how many people participate in the contests.

8. Potentially receive subsidies from various stakeholders to pay for launching, expanding, or sustaining the benefit provision.

   Social media could be used to help those who might provide subsidies to become more knowledgeable about and more impressed by what you are doing, receive more publicity for helping, and make those who contribute more excited about giving their financial support.

9. Directly create more demand for the firm's offerings due to the resulting social benefits.

   Social media and online contests involving lots of people are two of the most effective ways to locate better ways to create such a virtuous cycle.

As you can now better appreciate, adding millions of strangers who play many temporary, limited roles for gaining information, attracting attention, validating what's going on, encouraging better results, and identifying many previously unconsidered opportunities through online contests are just a few ways that the scale and scope of what you do could be multiplied far beyond what you can ask, think, or imagine. I believe that the social enterprises I've studied didn't make nearly enough use of strangers. In most cases, strangers didn't either add much to or detract from what occurred. They were simply ignored. 'Tis a pity!

What's the key lesson? *An organization that sincerely wants to accelerate its profitable growth can be helped by increasing the current level of social benefits by a much larger (more than 20 times) multiple than the profit increases that it gains from providing the social-benefit increases in ways that will attract millions of strangers to play many temporary, limited roles for attracting attention, validating what's going on, encouraging better results, and identifying previously unconsidered opportunities through online contests.*

<u>Your Lesson Eleven Assignments</u>

1. Identify how adding the actions of millions of strangers to supplement and amplify current stakeholders might help increase the quantity and types of social benefits provided to attract many more customers and offering and social-benefit end users, and more visible support from them for your organization's activities.

2. Identify how adding actions by millions of strangers might help increase purchases from customers who will pay premium prices and provide other economic benefits in support of the social purposes and your organization's ability to profit from this benefit expansion.

3. Evaluate how each social-benefit increase gained from carefully developing support from millions of strangers could affect each of the nine categories of potential sales and profit increases listed in this and the prior ten lessons in terms of attracting and obtaining more support from existing and new stakeholders who aren't strangers.

4. Search other industries to find practices that could be brought into your industry to greatly expand the contribution that millions of strangers make to the value of your social-benefit increases to customers and current and potential end users for offerings and social benefits.

5. Look beyond what anyone else has done to attract and beneficially engage millions of strangers in every conceivable temporary role that will expand social benefits by at least 400 times and company profits by 20 times or more.

Lesson Twelve

Co-Opt Competitors

Therefore, as through one man's offense
judgment came *to all men,*
resulting in condemnation,

even so through one Man's righteous act
the free gift came *to all men,*
resulting in justification of life.

— Romans 5:18 (NKJV)

Romans 5:18 (NKJV) refers to the sins of Adam and Eve, as well as the sacrifice of Jesus that permits us to gain Salvation. While none of us can hope to approach such spiritual significance through whatever our organizations do, we will often have a more profound effect than we realize. One such greater effect can be to stimulate competitors to follow our example.

This lesson considers ways to co-opt competitors. What I mean by "co-opt" is taking actions that give competitors little choice but to respond with complementary actions that enhance your organization's delivery of social benefits, as well as increase your profits. This lesson has deep roots in *Advanced Business for Innovation*, where you can learn from 50 lessons about engaging competitors to take actions that will advance an industry, as well as your own firm, through increased innovation.

Providing enormous increases in social benefits exerts influence in ways that mere money and formal power can never do. Let me outline five aspects of how such influence can work:

1. *Be a good example.* If what you do is so beneficial that you receive much approval and acclaim for doing so ... along with gaining a great deal of business ... competitors may feel that they have little choice but to emulate you.

   Here's a simple example: When Crest toothpaste became the first brand to contain fluoride and gained an endorsement from the American Dental Association, its competitors watched with interest. The airwaves were then filled with evidence provided by Crest that the cavity reductions were real, money would be saved at the dentist, and individuals wouldn't have to suffer so much in the dentist's chair. How could any competitor resist adding fluoride? And almost all of them followed Crest by doing so.

2. *Make a case for greater social benefits resulting from cooperation among competitors.* Some increases in social benefits can only be accomplished if compromises are made to create uniformly helpful practices in an industry.

   In the early days of the railroad industry in the United States, there was no standard for the width of railroad tracks. As a result, a freight or passenger car often couldn't run on the tracks of the next railroad. Long-haul freight frequently had to be unloaded, moved by horse-drawn vehicles, and then loaded onto a new railway car to accommodate such differences. Passengers also didn't enjoy frequently getting off and on trains toting their luggage.

   Consequently, water transportation flourished until such time as standard track gauges were adopted. With the universal switch, the cost of rail transportation plummeted, causing shippers and consumers to benefit from freer markets.

3. *Load extra burdens on customers of competitors that don't cooperate in increasing social benefits.* If the social benefit involves personal safety, the pressure can be substantial.

Roadside assistance can be very valuable whenever you have unexpected vehicle problems. Particularly late at night and in lonely locations, drivers experiencing breakdowns are eager to see a friendly face they can trust. Today, most motorists have access to cellular telephones. Some vehicles also have the capability of reaching an operator by pushing a button. In any case, you would like someone to come to you quickly ... while talking with someone who makes you feel less vulnerable.

In the United States, by far the biggest network of roadside service providers is directed by the American Automobile Association (AAA). Call AAA, and someone will probably get to you faster. For many years, AAA would only service its own members. Then, there were disturbing news reports of bad things happening to some of the people who weren't AAA members.

In response to such reports, AAA decided to start dispatching help to people who weren't members. Once help arrived, AAA told the tow truck operator that the individual who wasn't a member would have to pay the service provider directly ... usually a large expense. But safety needs were met. AAA had been co-opted into serving nonmembers.

AAA learned to place a call to those people about a week later to see if they were all right ... and to ask if they wanted to join AAA. Almost everyone did. Public-safety officials responded by instructing their patrols to only call AAA to help those with a roadside-vehicle problems.

Competitors tried to respond, but couldn't. The best they could do was to sponsor free roadside assistance on busy roads during peak traffic hours, a time when their help was less often needed. However, some people without AAA memberships benefited.

4. *Point to the immense value of social benefits that competitors cannot supply with different methods.* This information sharing is very powerful when safety is involved.

   In the United States, many people have tried to profit from gathering, storing, and distributing blood products. The Red Cross, by contrast, has insisted on running a nonprofit program that doesn't pay for blood or its products. Much advertising and many public-affairs notices have pointed out that unpaid donors are much less likely to have diseases (even though all blood is screened for such diseases) than are people who sell their blood. After hearing such information, many people imagine receiving blood from a drug addict who is HIV positive and are very upset by the possibility.

   The Red Cross has succeeded in increasing the amount of blood that's voluntarily provided through making these informational efforts, taking advantage of the preference for not obtaining blood from suspect sources to develop and promote more ways for those needing blood to provide for their own needs.

   In response, most blood-gathering organizations increased their emphasis on unpaid donors. It became much easier to donate. The blood supply grew safer and larger.

5. *Make it obvious when competitors are not cooperating in providing the social benefits.* Labels often provide a great way to do so. Increasingly, regulations determine what must be included on a label. With enough disclosure, noncompliance with some practice that delivers social benefits becomes obvious and encourages shifts. By lobbying government to add better disclosure, improved access to information can help encourage the provision of social benefits.

When recycling of glass bottles first became a major focus in the United States, laws required labels to note whether purchasers needed to pay a fee for the bottle and also if someone could return the bottle to receive the fee as a refund. Those who produced beverages without such recycling encouragement became very obvious, and environmentally concerned consumers spent less with such producers. Due to this pressure, most beverage makers eventually switched to recyclable bottles before laws made such practices mandatory.

Keeping these potential ways to influence competitors in mind, let's now consider what the opportunities are for co-opting competitors to gain advantages in the nine categories where providing substantially more social benefits can greatly increase company profits, as well:

1. Attract more customers and purchases because of customers wanting to support the social purpose.

   If your industry supplies more social benefits by cooperating with competitors to provide advantages over a functional substitute (say, railroads versus barges in being fuel efficient and reducing pollution), then it's natural for an industry association to set a standard, note who complies, and to publicize the public benefits. As a result, the industry should grow faster.

   Depending on the appeal of the social purpose, the effect of going from providing such benefits to a small portion of the total market (just your customers) to serving all potential customers can be enormous. If you receive public credit for leading your industry in this direction, your market share is likely to grow.

2. Obtain premium pricing due to the strength of customer desire to support the social purpose or to the marketing benefits received.

   This happy occurrence is most likely to be enjoyed when your industry's offerings can substitute for those of another industry that doesn't provide the social benefit and your organization gets the credit for tipping your industry in this direction.

3. Reduce costs by receiving volunteer help or reduced charges from suppliers who favor the purpose for the increased social benefits.

   If the volunteer help in some way increases the social benefits, then such cost reductions are likely to be gained. Imagine, for instance, that Amazon.com allowed customers from other online product sites to put reviews on its site without making any added effort. More reviews would be written and more people would pay attention to them. That's what Amazon.com did for Borders.com customers, and volunteerism rose while costs declined for Amazon.com and Borders.com.

   In terms of suppliers, the more you co-opt competitors the more likely that suppliers will do their best to accommodate all their good customers by providing the social benefits at lower cost. Gaining such support for providing this benefit may be important to co-opting competitors.

4. Experience fewer costs due to a higher drive among employees, partners, and suppliers for productivity, willingness to work harder in less favorable conditions, and demanding less in payments and benefits.

   Influencing industry-wide changes in behavior that expand social benefits will stimulate much more cooperation in all of these elements. The switch from making steel with raw materials in blast furnaces to using recycled steel as the major ingredient in electric furnaces and mini-mills provides a good example.

5. Avoid investments due to stakeholders doing more of such required investing.

When recycled newsprint first became a common paper ingredient, it was often hard to get enough newsprint at low cost. As the paper mills expanded their capacity, they found it advantageous to establish recycling networks that often functioned in church parking lots. The church parking lot had a big bin in it that publicly proclaimed that this church was doing its fair share to save trees. Conscientious churchgoers brought their newsprint to the gathering places at their own expense and didn't expect to be paid for it. The churches provided space and took only a small payment for their support. Not bad!

Competitors saw this approach being used and began placing their own bins. Everyone who used paper made from recycled newsprint benefited.

6. Increase sensitivity to improving cash flow by all stakeholders because of its effect on providing more for those who receive social benefits.

Such a benefit is certainly more likely to be enjoyed by an industry than by a single company. If a major stakeholder is a government entity, there's a better likelihood of obtaining subsidies and grants to encourage providing more of the social benefit.

7. Encourage innovative business models that build on the trust and preference for providing and receiving the social benefits.

The more universal the applicability of the business model, the more likely that people will pitch in to help. When I was young, a local charity raised money pretty effectively by passing the hat at Red Sox games. The charity still does that. Eventually, sponsors of televised games learned that they could get extra air time by donating to the charity whenever a Red Sox player did something outstanding. Donations grew.

Separately, the charity realized that those who had benefited from its activities made the best case for donations. The charity now sponsors a two-day bike ride involving thousands of people, most of whom are either beneficiaries of the charity or in the families of such beneficiaries. I was astonished to learn that the annual ride now raises almost $40 million, a huge sum for a local charity from one event. The Red Sox visibility for the charity opened this door, too.

I'm sure that many people also donate generously because they know someone whose life was saved by the work of this charity.

8. Potentially receive subsidies from various stakeholders to pay for launching, expanding, or sustaining the benefit provision.

Governments are obviously good candidates, as I mentioned before. As you can see from the examples I've provided, ordinary people will also chip in ... just for the good feeling they get from helping or from a sense of obligation for the social benefits that have been received.

9. Directly create more demand for the firm's offerings due to the resulting social benefits

The local-charity example supports this point, as well. By co-opting competitors among Red Sox advertisers, there's also an increased incentive to provide more kinds of social benefits ... due to the amplified effects of larger provision.

As you can now better appreciate, co-opting competitors is a lot like obtaining a free source of amplification of your marketing and sales efforts at essentially no cost.

What's the key lesson? *An organization that sincerely wants to accelerate its profitable growth can be helped by increasing the current level of social benefits by a much larger (more than 20 times) multiple than the profit increases that it gains from providing the social-benefit increases in ways that will co-opt competitors to participate.*

Your Lesson Twelve Assignments

1. Identify how co-opting competitors might help increase the quantity and types of social benefits provided to attract many more customers and offering and social-benefit end users, and more visible support from them for your organization.

2. Identify how co-opting competitors might help increase purchases from customers who will pay premium prices and provide other economic benefits in support of the social purposes and your organization's ability to profit from this benefit expansion.

3. Evaluate how each social-benefit increase from co-opting competitors could affect each of the nine categories of potential sales and profit increases listed in this and the prior eleven lessons in terms of attracting and obtaining more support from existing and new stakeholders who aren't competitors.

4. Search other industries to find practices that could be brought into your industry to greatly expand the contribution that co-opted competitors make to the value of your social-benefit increases to customers and current and potential end users for offerings and social benefits.

5. Look beyond what anyone else has done to co-opt competitors in every conceivable way that will expand social benefits by at least 400 times and company profits by 20 times or more.

Lesson Thirteen

Connect to Communities You Serve

"And do not seek what you should eat
or what you should drink,
nor have an anxious mind.
For all these things
the nations of the world seek after,
and your Father knows
that you need these things.
But seek the kingdom of God, and
all these things shall be added to you.
Do not fear, little flock,
for it is your Father's good pleasure
to give you the kingdom."

— Luke 12:29-32 (NKJV)

These verses from Luke 12:29-32 (NKJV) remind us that God will provide for the needs of those who follow Him in seeking to advance His Kingdom. Clearly, this is both an encouraging and a sobering message. Many companies have not done enough to support Christian organizations and activities in the communities that their firms serve.

Here is an area where company leaders can make a difference. Those who want to advance in a company will often emulate whatever the most senior people do. When such leaders are actively leading and serving in Christian organizations and activities, many others will do the same.

Creating value for communities is an activity where there can be more lip service (such as informally promising benefits) than practical results. Instead, organizations with jobs that can be brought into or taken away from a community are always being aggressively pursued by government authorities with offers of grants, subsidized loans, tax forgiveness, and legal exceptions the value of which almost always vastly exceed the economic benefit of what the companies ultimately bring to the community. In some cases, taking advantage of a community is unintentional on the company's part. In some other cases, it's a deliberate part of the company's way of doing business.

In that context, a firm that's been deliberately seeking to expand community benefits can expect a favorable reception to greatly increasing social benefits for many more stakeholders. When such increases are also done in ways that build God's Kingdom, there can be supernatural support for the new activities.

We consider in this lesson the effects of connections you make to the communities you serve through enhancing social benefits and profiting from doing so. As we have discussed before in *Business Basics* and *Advanced Business*, communities have substantial potential influence in a number of ways including these five:

1. Affecting the environment in which you do business

   This effect is true in both literal and psychological ways. Let's start with the literal. Your community probably has substantial authority to regulate what you do. If the relationship is a friendly one, the interests of all stakeholders can receive fair consideration and good compromises can be found that reduce costs and eliminate potential harm for everyone. If the relationship is a hostile one, solutions may be hard to find, expensive, and displeasing to almost everyone.

In a psychological sense, the relationship with the community can affect innovation, interest in and willingness for changing and improving, and the ease with which experimentation can occur. Imagine one company that's surrounded every day by angry picketers brandishing fists. Compare that psychological environment to one where community leaders are continually arriving to present awards for good behavior to the organization.

2. Spreading news about how your organization operates to those who live and work elsewhere

When checking out an organization, customers, end users, suppliers, partners, and other key stakeholders often visit the local communities where an organization does business to find out what people there have observed about how the business operates. Naturally, bad reports will spread faster and wider than good ones, so you can count on any ugly truths coming out. In these days of social-media fascination, the information spreads faster and wider than ever.

3. Amplifying awareness of the social benefits that your organization provides

In the simplest cases, this amplification will occur because many of the social benefits will be delivered directly to the local communities where you conduct business. People there will simply be describing what they have personally observed and experienced.

When I travel to medium-sized and smaller communities, I'm often struck by how people describe the most and least outstanding local organizations in terms of how many social benefits they are providing. Such sharing will occur without my asking. I believe it's because people are so touched to see a business go well beyond the minimum in providing for those in need. It also causes people to harshly judge organizations that don't do likewise.

4. Encouraging the formation of fruitful partnerships that accomplish more because of extraordinary contributions by the local community

   When a business develops a deserved reputation for enhancing social benefits in the community, those who live there will often add their own resources to increase how much can be accomplished. Several good examples can be found in Detroit, Michigan, where the city donated extremely attractive waterfront property for commercial development that otherwise would have been sold at very high prices. The city often granted long-term property-tax holidays to make being located there more attractive, and enhanced local police and fire services to make it safer to do business there.

5. Creating an environment in which the most effective local people seek relationships with your organization

   Think back to when you were younger. There were probably one or two firms that everyone thought would provide a dream job. When I was a youngster, working for the Disney organization in Southern California was such an example. To this day, Disney can often hire the cream of the crop at any wage or salary level, permitting much higher effectiveness and productivity at no higher cost.

While I could go on to identify more ways that increasing connections to the communities has potential influence on your results, let me stop at these five. Let's shift our attention now to how improved and expanded connections to the communities where you operate and serve might contribute to the nine major ways that doing more for social purposes often add to company profits:

1. Attract more customers and purchases because of customers wanting to support the social purpose.

   Local communities can make providing for the social purpose more visible, such as by sponsoring civic events that raise awareness or produce resources for the purpose. Many such activities can generate visibility that would cost tens of millions of dollars to duplicate through marketing and public relations efforts.

   If some of these events are directly tied to purchasing more of the firm's goods and services, then the connection can be made even more direct. Sometimes this benefit can be improved by making a special contribution to the social benefits tied to more people purchasing at a given time or in connection with a specific event.

2. Obtain premium pricing due to the strength of customer desire to support the social purpose or to the marketing benefits received.

   If people in the local communities are encouraged by and provided with opportunities to describe how your business's support for the social purpose has made a difference in individual lives, in families, in organizations, and in the entire community, the sense of satisfaction that customers receive from purchasing will make the premium price seem like a small disadvantage compared to the good feelings they gain by supporting you.

   You see this quite often in the United States now in a related way when discounters (such as Wal-Mart) want to move into a community. Many local residents will demonstrate on behalf of excluding Wal-Mart and its lower prices because of the large numbers of jobs that will be lost compared to continuing to pay higher prices to the local retailers and service providers who operate there now.

If you also support local employment for people who would ordinarily struggle to find jobs, you can benefit from both kinds of sympathy for helping others through paying higher prices.

3. Reduce costs by receiving volunteer help or reduced charges from suppliers who favor the purpose for the increased social benefits.

When your prestige is high in a community, volunteers and suppliers will generally target you as the organization they want to support. As a result, you can usually obtain more volunteers, pay suppliers less, and receive better service. My own experiences with analyzing how to improve supplier performance for Harvard University in dealing with Boston-area firms showed that there was a potential for the university to reduce costs from suppliers by 20 percent compared to what an average university in the area would pay due to the prestige factor.

Focused properly, having a reputation for being a provider of vast quantities of social benefits can be part of establishing higher prestige for your organization.

4. Experience fewer costs due to a higher drive among employees, partners, and suppliers for productivity, willingness to work harder in less favorable conditions, and demanding less in payments and benefits.

I am again reminded of surveys that were undertaken among white-collar university employees comparing what Harvard paid and how productive the people were to what occurred at other local universities. In some cases, Harvard was enjoying more than 100 percent more productivity. In Harvard's case, this was simply based on prestige. There wasn't as much of a social-benefit aspect to its productivity advantage. I believe that if prestige and enhanced social benefits could have been combined in this university, the advantage in employee productivity might well have been a multiple of the 100-percent advantage in some cases.

To the extent that the local community or government picks up some of the tasks that your business would otherwise have to do for itself, these aids become other sources of cost advantages.

5. Avoid investments due to stakeholders doing more of such required investing.

   As I mentioned in my earlier description of land donations in Detroit, Michigan, such investments by the local community can be quite large. In the case of Cambridge, Massachusetts, the local community has made a great effort to make it easy and attractive to conduct biotechnology research. As a result, the biotech firms there can operate at much lower cost than elsewhere in New England. By creating such a hub, the availability of talent was also improved.

6. Increase sensitivity to improving cash flow by all stakeholders because of its effect on providing more for those who receive social benefits.

   Communities are very interested in adding jobs, attracting glamorous companies and projects, and giving the impression of being progressive in supporting businesses. In many cases, a community can afford to make long-term investments in what you do that greatly improve your cash flow because of the associated benefits that your presence brings in affecting what other employers and organizations do. Even a community without much land or money to invest can provide substantial tax holidays that serve to greatly improve cash flow.

7. Encourage innovative business models that build on the trust and preference for providing and receiving the social benefits.

   I see this occur quite often in Rhode Island, the smallest state in the United States. Because people there don't move into or out of the state very often and unemployment is usually high, there's a strong sense of wanting to build the local community. The state has been blessed by many public-private partnerships that have created quite remarkable business models. Businesses appreciate that Rhode Island's small size reduces the cost of experimenting there ... while the impact on the local community and its support can be quite high. You also see this sort of collaboration in special enterprise zones around the world where the success of the whole zone is influenced by what other organizations do in that community.

   The opposite is also true. Where there is no strong sense of community, business-model innovation will receive little, or no, boost from community-business partnerships.

8. Potentially receive subsidies from various stakeholders to pay for launching, expanding, or sustaining the benefit provision.

   Where there are communities, there are also governments that can choose to subsidize whatever they want.

9. Directly create more demand for the firm's offerings due to the resulting social benefits.

   This potential is enormously expanded when many of the social benefits are received in the community. I'm reminded of many visits to Hershey, Pennsylvania, home of Hershey Foods, the

> candy manufacturer, which is mostly owned by a local charity. The charitable organization is a substantial part of the community, as is Hershey Foods, which provides much of the employment in the surrounding 40 miles. The manufacturing process leaves the air filled with delicious aromas. Hershey Foods also added an amusement park to improve community life. If you are within 100 miles of Hershey, Pennsylvania, you are going to run into some people who are pretty devoted to being sure the company prospers. The town has even named its streets to make the place even more charming for tourists who come to smell the chocolate ... and go home filled with tasty memories and bags of goodies.

As you can now better appreciate, connecting to the communities you serve through the social benefits you are so greatly enhancing is a particularly powerful tool for attracting more of the right kinds of attention and support.

What's the key lesson? *An organization that sincerely wants to accelerate its profitable growth can be helped by increasing the current level of social benefits by a much larger (more than 20 times) multiple than the profit increases that it gains from providing the social-benefit increases in ways that will better connect it with the communities it serves.*

Your Lesson Thirteen Assignments

1. Identify how connecting to communities you serve more effectively through emphasizing increased social benefits might, in turn, help increase the quantity and types of social benefits provided to attract many more customers and offering and social-benefit end users, and more visible support from them for your organization's activities.

2. Identify how connecting to communities you serve more effectively through emphasizing increased social benefits might help increase purchases from customers who will pay premium prices and provide other economic benefits in support of the social purposes and your organization's ability to profit from this benefit expansion.

3. Evaluate how each social-benefit increase from connecting to communities you serve more effectively through emphasizing increased social benefits could affect each of the nine categories of potential sales and profit increases listed in this and the prior twelve lessons in terms of attracting and obtaining more support from existing and new stakeholders.

4. Search other industries to find practices that could be brought into your industry to greatly expand the contribution that connecting to communities you serve more effectively through emphasizing increased social benefits makes to the value of your social-benefit increases to customers and current and potential end users for offerings and social benefits.

5. Look beyond what anyone else has done to connect with communities you serve more effectively through emphasizing increased social benefits in every conceivable way that will expand social benefits by at least 400 times and company profits by 20 times or more.

Lesson Fourteen

Attract Government Support

For unto us a Child is born,
Unto us a Son is given;
And the government will be upon His shoulder.
And His name will be called
Wonderful, Counselor, Mighty God,
Everlasting Father, Prince of Peace.
Of the increase of His *government and peace*
There will be *no end,*
Upon the throne of David and over His kingdom,
To order it and establish it with judgment and justice
From that time forward, even forever.
The zeal of the L*ORD* *of hosts will perform this.*

— Isaiah 9:6-7 (NKJV)

Many people are conflicted in their views about government. Such people may want their government to perform certain functions well, such as keeping the peace. However, the same people may resent being stopped by a police officer for speeding while driving in their vehicles. With such a "what's in it for me?" view of personal benefits and costs associated with government, it's easy for even faithful believers to forget that government belongs, as everything else does, to Jesus. When we take that perspective, we realize that being in positive partnership with government to expand His Kingdom is a righteous activity, one with spiritual, as well as earthly, rewards.

In this lesson, we look at where most social enterprises begin with seeking resources: attracting government support. Since nations vary a lot in how they are organized, this discussion will have to be a bit generic. Please adjust the comments to fit with the government structure of the nations in which you are based and do business.

There are a number of highly appropriate reasons to seek government support beyond seeing this as a source of funding with deep pockets. Let me summarize the five most important reasons:

1. The social benefits that you want to provide may have value to governments either for reducing costs that they incur or in providing revenue that they would not otherwise receive.

   For example, if your expansion of social benefits creates many jobs for the chronically unemployed, governments will pay out less for unemployment benefits and providing income support, while also receiving more tax revenues from income and value-added tax payments.

2. Expanding your approach to increasing social benefits to also provide more cost and revenue benefits for governments may be possible without reducing benefits for anyone else.

   In such an instance, governments may want to encourage you to do more to assist them. This encouragement might take tangible form through grants to conduct experiments, subsidies to perform activities that otherwise wouldn't be affordable by you, or tax incentives to accomplish certain results. Intangible support might include public statements encouraging people to participate in your programs.

3. Political realities in many nations mean that certain services have to be provided regardless of how expensive and difficult

they are. If you can find far more effective and efficient ways to perform some of those services, governments may be able to reduce or eliminate what they are doing that's expensive and politically embarrassing.

I think of monitoring and supervising paroled drug addicts and sex offenders as such an activity. Almost all of such individuals are going to commit these crimes again. The harm they cause is usually impossible to completely remedy and such occurrences make governments look bad. Finding a way to reduce the rate of recidivism would be a great social benefit to provide. Governments would especially welcome some effective approach that also reduced how much had to be done with these individuals after they are paroled.

4. Governments like to increase their appeal to new and existing businesses. If some of the social benefits you expand have a large positive influence on such appeals, there are prestige reasons, in addition to economic ones, for supporting what you are doing.

   As an example, consider ways to provide quick and effective training in types of work for which there is a scarcity of workers. In a rapidly growing field such as biotechnology, providing such an expanded social benefit could be enormously valuable in terms of attracting and retaining employers, adding great jobs, and improving the health and productivity of individuals in the society.

5. If some pervasive problem limits the habitability and attractiveness of a given geographic area, governments may be quite eager to encourage your solution that eases or eliminates the problem.

For instance, in many parts of the world there's a shortage of clean water for drinking and bathing. Until the clean water supply is expanded at a reasonable cost, such areas won't see much growth in the health of their citizens, their economies, and in individual incomes. Greatly multiplying the availability of such water at lower-than-current costs would be of immense interest to many governments whose inhabitants operate under such limitations.

While I could go on to identify more ways that government support could be attracted, I'll stop at these five. However, I encourage you to keep thinking about other ways that might fit your business.

Let's shift our focus now to how attracting government support could contribute to the nine major ways that serving social purposes often add to company profits:

1. Attract more customers and purchases because of customers wanting to support the social purpose.

   Here we are often dealing with the social purpose's appeal to government wanting to encourage expansion of the customer and purchase base. Let me give you two examples.

   Regulations and legislation are two ways that governments can shift consumption. For instance, here in the United States the Obama administration announced in 2012 a new rule that all vehicles will have to provide average fuel economy of 57.5 miles per gallon by 2025. Such a target cannot be met without employing battery technology as one source of power, usually through being charged by electricity that can be generated by coal and natural gas, both of which are in great supply. Those who provide such vehicles now will see a huge expansion in their market as 2025 approaches. In such a case, it's the government's desire to support the social purpose of relying less on oil for transportation that's driving (pun intended) the opportunity to attract more customers and purchases.

Governments can also provide subsidies for purchasers who choose offerings that include the most socially beneficial solutions, either through tax reductions or direct payments. For instance, such an approach is often taken for encouraging solar-power generation and usage.

2. Obtain premium pricing due to the strength of customer desire to support the social purpose or to the marketing benefits received.

To the extent that purchases or usage of your offerings are subsidized by the government, your prices can be higher.

Such subsidies can also come in the form of help, instead of direct payments. For instance, widespread use of batteries in vehicles will mean that there will need to be many places where batteries can be recharged while parked during travel. Governments might pay to put in such charging stations as a way to encourage use of the new offerings. Or governments can require electricity-generating and -transmission firms to put in large numbers of such stations.

3. Reduce costs by receiving volunteer help or reduced charges from suppliers who favor the purpose for the increased social benefits.

Governments can increase how much volunteer help is available by chartering nonprofit organizations to operate in support of what you do, holding "official" events that encourage people to volunteer in certain ways, and making efforts to attract volunteers through public messages. In some cases, governments also provide subsidies for nonprofit organizations that muster lots of volunteers. In a few cases, governments may even establish their own volunteer enterprises that can assist your organization in providing more social benefits.

4. Experience fewer costs due to a higher drive among employees, partners, and suppliers for productivity, willingness to work harder in less favorable conditions, and demanding less in payments and benefits.

   If governments create a sense of social priority for what you are doing, such lower-cost results can follow. I recently read a history of the American space program between the time of announcing the goal to go to the moon with men and reaching there. I was struck by how many sacrifices were made by individuals and organizations to accomplish something where the technology wasn't yet ready, but the social priority was high. There's no reason why a similar sense of urgency and priority can't be attached to some social purpose that excites a government and its citizens.

   Even without such support, simply spotlighting what is being accomplished can create a sense of pride among employees and suppliers, as well as a desire to achieve even more that can lead to higher productivity and lower costs.

5. Avoid investments due to stakeholders doing more of such required investing.

   Governments have traditionally played this role for funding investments that private enterprise would have no economic incentive to make. If you can build a case that the social benefits you will expand are valuable enough to that government, chances are good that it can help you avoid investments. Sometimes this support can only be received by providing access to government-guaranteed loans that reduce interest costs, so the subsidy may be slight in such cases.

Changing existing regulations and legislation to eliminate barriers to providing new forms of offerings can be a very big help, especially where the providers of the older form of offerings might try to block a newer one by insisting on unneeded activities, such as inspections that are costly but don't help improve performance.

6. Increase sensitivity to improving cash flow by all stakeholders because of its effect on providing more for those who receive social benefits.

   Governments often have "off-the-balance-sheet" ways to assist. When such are involved (as through guarantees, providing access to government bond markets, etc.), governments are usually relatively insensitive about when they make their financial contribution, potentially providing deep pockets in the beginning of your new activity, making the overall cash flow much better.

7. Encourage innovative business models that build on the trust and preference for providing and receiving the social benefits.

   Governments can often encourage through the process of offering contracts to develop and provide experimental solutions. I'm reminded of the current approach by NASA in the United States to providing contracts for supplying the International Space Station to rocket producers. These contracts have encouraged many fine developments in business models for low-cost space transportation.

8. Potentially receive subsidies from various stakeholders to pay for launching, expanding, or sustaining the benefit provision.

   Governments can do so both directly (with subsidies) and indirectly (by requiring that certain offerings be used, such as with ethanol in gasoline in the United States). In the developing world, governments may be able to attract funds for such expenditures from international agencies and governments in developed countries.

9. Directly create more demand for the firm's offerings due to the resulting social benefits.

   Governments are so inefficient in performing some tasks that it's highly likely that such opportunities can be found. For instance, the cost of obtaining income-tax revenue from 240 million of the 300-plus million citizens and residents in the United States exceeds the collected amount by a wide margin. I can imagine a day when private companies will propose new ways to generate such tax revenue less expensively that will, in turn, improve the economic health of those who are burdened now by the inefficiencies of providing the required reports and filings.

   Another example involves prisoners. The average cost in the United States per prisoner was estimated to be between $60,000 and $100,000 a year in 2015. Clearly, a program that made many of such people less dangerous when freed, so that they didn't need to be in prison as long, could save a lot of money and create more value for society.

   During the first economic recovery in the 21st century, the United States federal government spent over $1,000,000 for each net new job created. Surely, some private program could have generated such jobs at a much lower cost and provided much more employment.

As you can now better appreciate, attracting government support for the social benefits you are so greatly enhancing is a particularly good potential source for obtaining more of the right kinds of attention and support.

What's the key lesson? *An organization that sincerely wants to accelerate its profitable growth can be helped by increasing the current level of social benefits by a much larger (more than 20 times) multiple than the profit increases that it gains from providing the social-benefit increases in ways that attract government support.*

Your Lesson Fourteen Assignments

1. Identify how attracting government support through emphasizing increased social benefits might, in turn, help increase the quantity and types of social benefits provided to attract many more customers and offering and social-benefit end users, and more visible support from them for your organization.

2. Identify how attracting government support through emphasizing increased social benefits might help increase purchases from customers who will pay premium prices and provide other economic benefits in support of the social purposes and your organization's ability to profit from this benefit expansion.

3. Evaluate how each social-benefit increase from attracting government support through emphasizing increased social benefits could affect each of the nine categories of potential sales and profit increases listed in this and the prior thirteen lessons in terms of attracting and obtaining more support from existing and new stakeholders.

4. Search other industries to find practices that could be brought into your industry to greatly expand the contribution that attracting government support through emphasizing increased social benefits makes to the value of your social-benefit increases to customers and current and potential end users for offerings and social benefits.

5. Look beyond what anyone else has done to attract government support through emphasizing increased social benefits in every conceivable way that will expand social benefits by at least 400 times and company profits by 20 times or more.

Lesson Fifteen

Interest and Enlist Experts

The heart of the prudent acquires knowledge,
And the ear of the wise seeks knowledge.
A man's gift makes room for him,
And brings him before great men.

— Proverbs 18:15-16 (NKJV)

Proverbs 18:15-16 (NKJV) contains several pearls of wisdom. First, someone who is prudent feels a heart-felt desire to acquire knowledge. Such a heart should be found in both those who seek and those who provide Godly advice. Second, wise people listen to advice to gain knowledge. Such hearers don't think that "they know it all." If both activities are done well, someone who has developed useful knowledge will eventually be asked to share it with those who are then deemed to be the greatest. Such greatly esteemed hearers are going to be those who are doing the most to advance God's Kingdom. Hopefully, your company will contain many of such great ones.

This lesson investigates how to have the right kind of relationship with a group of people that isn't often considered in books about businesses improving social benefits: experts. I see a number of potentially valuable contributions by experts; six of the most important of these potential contributions are summarized here:

1. Experts or their students may have experimented with some of the potential ways that social benefits can be increased by 400 times. Such experiments can reveal important lessons for what to do, as well as what to avoid doing. Building from what was learned during such experiments, experts or their students may also be able to suggest improvements to test in new experiments that could greatly accelerate providing more social benefits.

2. Many people who are considering how much support to provide for what you are doing will probably consult experts to find out how they view your plans. If the experts report not having been consulted or say your ideas make no sense to them, your credibility and ability to attract broader support will be harmed.

3. When journalists write about your plans and actions, they will seek experts to comment. Since some journalists like nothing better than to stir up controversy, even where there is none, they are likely to go hunting for experts who can point out obvious flaws in what you are planning to do or how you are implementing. If you have already interested and enlisted many experts and made adjustments based on what you have learned from them, such critiques will be much more limited and less damaging to your credibility.

4. Providing a sense that experts are interested in and engaged by this project will also stir public interest and government support. To the extent such stakeholders are important to the ultimate accomplishment of increasing social benefits by 400 times, you will enjoy more of the stakeholders' interest and support, as well.

5. Experts may also be able to propose ways of involving other stakeholder groups that your own work might not uncover.

For instance, experts in online contests can help you make such contests more effective. Other experts might have insights into how to persuade more people to volunteer and to donate money for expanding social benefits.

6. Experts who write about the project can also help to engage the interest of knowledgeable people who don't normally work in these fields, but whose expertise could be applied in quite valuable ways.

While I could go on to identify more ways that expert help could be attracted and used effectively, I'll stop at these six. As you can see, experts can help with experience, knowledge, and credibility.

Let's shift our focus now to how interesting and enlisting experts could contribute to the nine major ways that serving social purposes often add to company profits:

1. Attract more customers and purchases because of customers wanting to support the social purpose.

   The more credible customers see the promise of many more social benefits being produced, the more purchases and new customers will be attracted. Experts may also be helpful in developing ways to increase customer interest in providing more of the social benefits through their purchases.

2. Obtain premium pricing due to the strength of customer desire to support the social purpose or to the marketing benefits received.

   Just providing many more social benefits doesn't ensure that customers will want to pay premium prices. Marketing experts might be quite helpful in identifying what to emphasize about expanding social benefits that will most incline customers to pay more as part of their contribution to achieving the results.

3. Reduce costs by receiving volunteer help or reduced charges from suppliers who favor the purpose for the increased social benefits.

   Once again, credibility from the experts can be quite a help. If individuals and suppliers are feeling more assured that their contributions will make an important difference, they will be more eager to participate. Such contributors will gain an enhanced sense of self-worth that's worth a lot more than money to many. Experts in attracting volunteers can also be quite useful.

4. Experience fewer costs due to a higher drive among employees, partners, and suppliers for productivity, willingness to work harder in less favorable conditions, and demanding less in payments and benefits.

   Imagine that the social benefits being increased help young children with once-incurable cancer to survive and thrive. The thought of doing something for such children would move most hearts. Yet, it can be hard to credit some vague promise that good results will follow without having confirmation from those experts who should best be in a position to know.

5. Avoid investments due to stakeholders doing more of such required investing.

   Here's another place where credibility will make a big difference in how much stakeholder willingness to bear investment costs there will be.

6. Increase sensitivity to improving cash flow by all stakeholders because of its effect on providing more for those who receive social benefits.

   Credibility provided by experts will again play a key role, particularly if governments are to provide some funding.

7. Encourage innovative business models that build on the trust and preference for providing and receiving the social benefits.

   Experts can point the way to and help develop practices that can become building blocks for innovative business models.

8. Potentially receive subsidies from various stakeholders to pay for launching, expanding, or sustaining the benefit provision.

   Subsidies are often tied to ways of measuring what's being accomplished and the credibility of such measurements. Experts can be quite helpful in both dimensions.

9. Directly create more demand for the firm's offerings due to the resulting social benefits.

   Experts can be exceptionally useful in this regard by pointing out ways that an improvement in one activity can feed into creating more resources and positive results in other aspects of increasing social benefits.

What's the key lesson? *An organization that sincerely wants to accelerate its profitable growth can be helped by increasing the current level of social benefits by a much larger (more than 20 times) multiple than the profit increases that it gains from providing the social-benefit expansions in ways that interest and enlist the help of experts.*

Your Lesson Fifteen Assignments

1. Identify how interesting and enlisting experts to work on increasing social benefits might, in turn, help expand the quantity and types of social benefits provided to attract many more customers and offering and social-benefit end users, and more visible support from them for your organization's activities.

2. Identify how interesting and enlisting experts to work on increasing social benefits might help expand purchases from customers who will pay premium prices and provide other economic benefits in support of the social purposes and your organization's ability to profit from this benefit expansion.

3. Evaluate how each social-benefit increase from interesting and enlisting experts to work on increasing social benefits could affect each of the nine categories of potential sales and profit increases listed in this and the prior fourteen lessons in terms of attracting and obtaining more support from existing and new stakeholders.

4. Search other industries to find practices that could be brought into your industry to greatly expand the contribution that interesting and enlisting experts to work on increasing social benefits make to the value of your social-benefit increases to current and potential end users for offerings and social benefits.

5. Look beyond what anyone else has done to interest and enlist experts to work on increasing social benefits by at least 400 times and company profits by 20 times or more.

Lesson Sixteen

Gain Support from Authorities

So they came to Jerusalem.
Then Jesus went into the temple and
began to drive out those
who bought and sold in the temple,
and overturned the tables of the money changers
and the seats of those who sold doves.
And He would not allow anyone
to carry wares through the temple.
Then He taught, saying to them,
"Is it not written, 'My house shall be called
a house of prayer for all nations'?
But you have made it a 'den of thieves.'"

And the scribes and chief priests heard it
and sought how they might destroy Him;
for they feared Him, because all the people
were astonished at His teaching.
When evening had come, He went out of the city.

Then they came again to Jerusalem.
And as He was walking in the temple,
the chief priests, the scribes, and
the elders came to Him. And they said to Him,
"By what authority are You doing these things?
And who gave You this authority to do these things?"

— Mark 11:15-19, 27-28 (NKJV)

The events described in Mark 11:15-19, 27-28 (NKJV) occurred just after Jesus arrived in Jerusalem on Palm Sunday. The chief priests were in charge of the Temple, and they were unused to anyone else acting with authority there. When Jesus returned to the Temple after "cleaning house," the chief priests, the scribes, and the elders of the Temple challenged His actions in rooting out commerce by asking Jesus the source of His authority. Notice that they did this even though Jesus had cited the authority of Scripture at the time of His cleansing of the Temple. Since the people were supportive of Jesus at this point, these challengers were trying to undermine His strength so that they could eventually reassert their temporal authority. Jesus refused to answer the question unless the challengers first answered his question about whether the baptism of John was from heaven or from men.

As you can see from this example, a sustained ability to accomplish results eventually relies on having legitimate authority. Otherwise, support will dwindle away. In many cases such authority comes from formal sources (such as the Bible), or entities (such as governments), but in other cases the authority of an individual rests in the eyes of the beholders and ears of the hearers as they judge what they notice.

Having just finished a lesson concerning experts, your first reaction to this lesson may be to wonder how individuals who are authorities are different from experts. Let me explain the distinction that I have in mind.

Experts are those with superior information, knowledge, skills, and experience who can add value to a solution by providing an enhancement. In most cases, however, people with such valuable information, knowledge, skills, and experience aren't well known outside their fields. Thus, if you want help with developing a nanotechnology solution for providing some new social benefit, the person who adds that expertise may well be initially unknown to you before conducting a search for the right expert.

By contrast, an authority is someone who commands instant recognition in terms of face, appearance, name, or credentials such that almost every stakeholder would be heavily influenced by whatever the person has to say about your breakthrough, even if he or she has no specific information, knowledge, skills, and experience that can add any value. Sticking with the nanotechnology point, such an authority could be a Nobel Prize winner for medicine who is known for successful vaccine development but who has not very well-founded opinions about the advisability of humans being exposed to artificial substances that more easily reach the blood stream through breathing and contact with skin. Such an authority might express doubts about your breakthrough solution that are completely wrong, but the doubts could still be such a substantial influence that your breakthrough would be rejected or greatly limited in influence with some people.

Something like this has already happened to developing medicines in the United States. One of the ways that new medicines are tested is by loading animals with hundreds of times the exposure that humans would ever receive to see what happens. Some authorities once opined that it was dangerous to allow a single human to ever be exposed to any substance that created any cancer in such overloaded animals. Consequently, many trials of medicines have been stopped by an American law that was based on the views of such authorities. Many experts would argue that's a big mistake because interactions with substances differ from one species to another, and the levels that humans receive would be much smaller.

I pray that you now appreciate the distinction that I am making between experts and authorities.

Let's look at the potential influence of authorities. I see three primary ways that authorities might affect a breakthrough solution that expands social benefits by at least 400 times:

1. By stating a view that causes others to be skeptical of or to oppose your breakthrough (as described in the nanotechnology example I just shared)
2. Raising irrelevant or unimportant questions that cannot be easily answered so that delays and expenses are incurred to develop and interpret the appropriate information
3. Endorsing what is being proposed so that the solution becomes available sooner and is employed by more people who need the benefits

Realize that for any given topic or opinion, different authorities may line up for, against, or neutrally. Since there are many potential authorities who could influence stakeholders, you need to explain the facts to a good number of the more credible authorities so that they will come to an accurate conclusion about your breakthrough.

Assuming that you develop such support from many of the most esteemed authorities, what are the impacts on profits? Let's examine each element on our familiar list once again.

1. Attract more customers and purchases because of customers wanting to support the social purpose.

   The more credibility that customers assign to the promise of many more social benefits being provided, the more purchases will occur and new customers be attracted. The views of authorities can expand news coverage of and increase public interest in your breakthrough. To the extent that customers and end users view a given authority as dependable, a positive view by that authority can easily turn into immediate and continuing use of whatever you offer.

2. Obtain premium pricing due to the strength of customer desire to support the social purpose or to the marketing benefits received.

As I noted in the prior lesson, just providing many social benefits doesn't ensure that customers will want to pay premium prices. Authorities who endorse your breakthrough and also support the idea that it's constructive to pay more for offerings as a way of contributing to the desirable results can move customers and end users to greatly reduce their normal sensitivity to paying higher prices.

I believe that such a result has occurred with many families that emphasize organic foods. Although the main advantage of eating organic is to avoid ingesting dangerous substances such as pesticides, herbicides, and other toxins, few people have any sense of what such advantages are worth in financial terms. Should you pay 1 percent more? How about 40 percent? The uncertainty has undoubtedly contributed to many people paying quite high price premiums for organic foods.

3. Reduce costs by receiving volunteer help or reduced charges from suppliers who favor the purpose for the increased social benefits.

   Once again, authorities can be quite a help. If individuals and suppliers are certain that their contributions of time and effort will make an important difference to providing more social benefits that they care about, they will be eager to participate. Volunteers and suppliers will gain an enhanced sense of self-worth that many value more than money. Authorities may also play a role in increasing how many people feel encouraged to learn about, to care about, and to support providing the breakthrough level of social benefits.

4. Experience fewer costs due to a higher drive among employees, partners, and suppliers for productivity, willingness to work harder in less favorable conditions, and demanding less in payments and benefits.

If the benefits are easy to appreciate and move hearts, many more authorities will be interested in attracting attention to the "cause." In most cases, such interest will translate into larger interest in expanding productivity, greater willingness to work hard in less favorable conditions, and demanding less in payments and benefits.

I believe that something like this effect is part of Aravind's success. Hardly anyone opposes the idea of making eye care available to more people who cannot afford it ... or at lower cost to those who can pay. Consequently, Aravind receives many visitors who are prominent in their fields who come to see what's being done. I'm sure that many of the staff and patients find themselves encouraged by meeting these authorities during such visits.

Something similar occurs at the offices of the Children's Television Network, best known for its award-winning show Sesame Street that teaches youngsters basic reading and math skills. The organization receives many offers from well-known performers to volunteer their services or to be paid a pittance for appearing in an episode. When these authorities arrive for a shooting, staff members and volunteers enjoy meeting these performers, making such workers more willing to do whatever it takes for Sesame Street to be more successful, even at their own expense.

5. Avoid investments due to stakeholders doing more of such required investing.

Many authorities make it a regular practice to spend time supporting various social causes. In the course of doing so, such authorities often work with organizations that hire them to appear in advertisements or to make speeches or publicity appearances. In such cases, an authority may be able to introduce you to other organizations she or he knows that would be interested in providing investment or other kinds of support for what you do.

6. Increase sensitivity to improving cash flow by all stakeholders because of its effect on providing more for those who receive social benefits.

   Authorities might well lend their voices to support the idea of customers paying sooner or suppliers being paid more slowly, as part of making more of the social benefits available to more people. As an example, I have seen authorities make formal pitches for people to take on some cash-flow burdens where the benefits were substantial for beneficiaries and stakeholders were going to provide a certain level of cash at some point.

7. Encourage innovative business models that build on the trust and preference for providing and receiving the social benefits.

   To the extent that authorities have their own followers, connecting with the authorities may provide formal opportunities to make permanent connections with such followers. For instance, an authority might offer a special opportunity to meet him or her to those who performed certain tasks on behalf of the breakthrough activity.

8. Potentially receive subsidies from various stakeholders to pay for launching, expanding, or sustaining the benefit provision.

   Some authorities are associated with organizations that are themselves authoritative, such as the American Dental Association. Many times such organizations won't become involved in supporting something unless a prominent authority pushes them to do so. There may also be a need for the organization to fund any independent investigations that it does, which would act as subsidies for your own research and marketing activities.

9. Directly create more demand for the firm's offerings due to the resulting social benefits

   Some social benefits are so popular to provide that almost every authority wants to become involved and help in some way. When that occurs, there's virtually unlimited potential to expand in the other eight dimensions of profit improvement, increasing the likelihood that an expanding beneficial cycle of interest being created. The famous advertising campaign for dairy farmers in the United States called "Got Milk?" featured well-known people sporting a milk mustache indicating that they were milk drinkers. These people volunteered their time so the only cost was for the photography. Substantial news coverage of the ads meant that such images received many free placements and viewings. The result was to expand the overall consumption of milk, something that had not happened in some years. With the ads more than paying for themselves by expanding consumption, the association could have continued to expand its reach with other programs ... but it didn't do so. Only doing the advertising campaign was a mistake in my view.

Okay, you are probably convinced that you should gain support from authorities. How should you do so?

Before approaching authorities, you already need to have clear evidence for the value of how you intend to expand social benefits by 400 times. With that information in hand, you should next conduct research to find all those who have ever expressed public opinions about the importance of such benefits. It's from among such people that you are most likely to find supportive authorities. Approach them through any credible intermediaries who know you both. Then ask for the authority's help in evaluating how appropriate your approach is. In other words, treat the authorities as if they are experts, even if they are not. Take whatever comments you receive seriously and look into what is observed. If possible, find the answers or tell the person why it's not practical to answer. Ask for suggestions. The authority may well have a solution that you have not thought of. After you have answers, ask for advice about the best way to increase awareness of the information. Chances are pretty good that you'll draw an endorsement on the spot and possibly some volunteer support.

After you have added someone as a supportive authority, ask for suggestions of other authorities to contact. Each authority knows dozens of others well. Ask for personal introductions. Chances are you'll obtain such introductions, and they will lead to adding other supportive authorities.

If an authority turns out to be opposed, ask for suggestions about how to overcome whatever concerns are expressed. The authority may well have a good point that will save much pain and agony. In addition, doing something about the concern will probably lead to your obtaining this person as a supportive authority who will be eager to tell others that he or she caused you to make an improvement.

After you have quite a few authorities on your side, ask for thoughts about who the most influential critics and opponents are likely to be and what concerns these people may have. Investigate what you can do to deal with these concerns. Then approach these potential opponents to ask for their advice concerning how to improve what you are going to offer. Most people will be flattered to hear from you about how to improve. Such people will often feel as if you are seeing them as experts, rather than just as authorities.

Take these concerns most seriously. Their issues can sink your boat (or at least your breakthrough solution).

When you think you've covered all the ground you can with authorities and responded appropriately, go public with their observations and support. You'll be glad you did!

What's the key lesson? *An organization that sincerely wants to accelerate its profitable growth can be helped by increasing the current level of social benefits by a much larger (more than 20 times) multiple than the profit increases that it gains from providing the social-benefit expansions in ways that gain support from authorities.*

Your Lesson Sixteen Assignments

1. Identify how gaining support from authorities for your way of increasing social benefits might, in turn, help expand the quantity and types of social benefits provided to attract many more customers and offering and social-benefit end users, and more visible support from them for your organization.

2. Identify how gaining support from authorities for your way of increasing social benefits might help expand purchases from customers who will pay premium prices and provide other economic benefits in support of the social purposes and your organization's ability to profit from this benefit expansion.

3. Evaluate how each social-benefit increase from gaining support from authorities for your way of increasing social benefits could affect each of the nine categories of potential sales and profit increases listed in this and the prior fifteen lessons in terms of attracting and obtaining more support from existing and new stakeholders.

4. Search other industries to find practices that could be brought into your industry to greatly expand the contribution that gaining support from authorities for your way of increasing social benefits makes to the value of your social-benefit increases to customers and current and potential end users for offerings and social benefits.

5. Look beyond what anyone else has done to gain support from authorities for your way of increasing social benefits by at least 400 times and company profits by 20 times or more.

Lesson Seventeen

Gain Support from Foundations

And certain men *came down*
from Judea and taught the brethren,
"Unless you are circumcised according to
the custom of Moses, you cannot be saved."

Therefore, when Paul and Barnabas had
no small dissension and dispute with them,
they determined that Paul and Barnabas and
certain others of them should go up to Jerusalem,
to the apostles and elders, about this question.

So, being sent on their way by the church,
they passed through Phoenicia and Samaria,
describing the conversion of the Gentiles;
and they caused great joy to all the brethren.

And when they had come to Jerusalem,
they were received by the church and
the apostles and the elders; and
they reported all things that
God had done with them.

— Acts 15:1-4 (NKJV)

Even among those highly dedicated to a certain end, as in the case of Acts 15:1-4 (NKJV) concerning Gentiles coming to faith, there can be major differences of opinion. When such disputes occur, there's a need for organizations with credibility and well-established reputations for objectivity to play a role. Here, the apostles and elders in Jerusalem were in a good position to consider the evidence of Paul and Barnabas in spreading the Gospel to Gentiles and the views of Christian Pharisees. This was an important moment for one view to emerge, one view that everyone could accept as being correct. Similarly, if there are either potential or actual serious disagreements about your approach to expanding social benefits, such organizations can be a big help in creating resolutions. Consider foundations as being one such possible type of organization for such purposes.

Foundations are organizations that accept donations or have substantial endowments that permit long-term focus on achieving socially beneficial goals. A foundation can contribute to accomplishing a social purpose in any of the following four ways:

1. By expressing selfless recognition for improvements that commands wide attention — Perhaps the most famous of such organizations is the Nobel Foundation that sponsors and provides annual prizes for outstanding achievements in various areas of science and social science, as well as for advancing peace. Think of the primary contribution as *validating the best work*.
2. By sponsoring the most advanced work in a given field that all societies are depending on for some major improvement — Today, that distinction might apply to the work of the Gates Foundation in supplying vaccines. Think of the primary contribution of this method as *advancing the best work faster* than would otherwise occur.
3. By forming the core of a popular cause to accomplish some specific purpose by drawing on as many of society's resources as possible — In the 1950s, the March of Dimes Foundation played that role in raising the money and directing research

for finding a polio vaccine and making that vaccine widely available. Think of the primary contribution of this method as providing *leadership for obtaining broad support.*

4. By sustaining an important activity that would otherwise be ignored by a society that places little immediate importance on what is being done — Today, this role is played by the Templeton Foundation in its work to find ways for spiritual faith and science to better engage with one another. Think of the primary contribution of this method as *changing the public agenda* by concentrating resources where otherwise either few or none would be applied.

Assuming that you develop such support from the most desirable foundations in terms of these four ways of contributing to public purposes, what are the impacts on profits? Let's examine each element on our familiar list:

1. Attract more customers and purchases because of customers wanting to support the social purpose.

   Clearly, all four ways of contributing can help here. If your approach is validated as being the best, more people will purchase to support it. If some people need what you offer but cannot afford it, a foundation may purchase and supply what you offer to some of them. Or, if it's not economic to do some advanced work, a foundation of this sort may fund some or all of such advanced work ... enabling you to provide improved offerings. If a cause is connected to what you do, such a foundation can bring sustained image and awareness to your offerings that would be expensive and difficult to supply for yourself. If what you are doing isn't on the public agenda, a foundation may help you through lean times until the public agenda switches so that you can benefit from having more customers and sales.

2. Obtain premium pricing due to the strength of customer desire to support the social purpose or to the marketing benefits received.

   I think the analysis of the four kinds of contribution here is virtually identical to point 1, so I won't elaborate except to point out that foundation support that enhances the actual performance of your offerings will, in many cases, be more helpful in generating a profit premium than in attracting more customers and sales.

3. Reduce costs by receiving volunteer help or reduced charges from suppliers who favor the purpose for the increased social benefits.

   I believe that it's when foundations provide leadership for attracting broad support that this kind of benefit will be received. There may also be some instances where the validation support can help, depending on how popular the social benefit is that you are choosing to advance.

4. Experience fewer costs due to a higher drive among employees, partners, and suppliers for productivity, willingness to work harder in less favorable conditions, and demanding less in payments and benefits.

   To me, the analysis here is similar to that for point 3.

5. Avoid investments due to stakeholders doing more of such required investing.

   The four foundation roles all offer the potential to enhance how much funding is gained from others, but especially in the second and fourth roles.

6. Increase sensitivity to improving cash flow by all stakeholders because of its effect on providing more for those who receive social benefits.

   Foundations are not only a great source of cash; they are usually required to part with a fair amount of it each year under the rules of where they are chartered. You can compete with other grant applicants for cash that will improve your cash flow. Because your productivity in using resources will be so high, you should have a great advantage in seeking such resources.

7. Encourage innovative business models that build on the trust and preference for providing and receiving the social benefits.

   Foundations in all four roles can improve the effectiveness of such innovations by validating, encouraging, funding, and publicizing them.

8. Potentially receive subsidies from various stakeholders to pay for launching, expanding, or sustaining the benefit provision.

   Foundation support can prove to be even more influential than the views of experts and authorities for causing potential subsidy providers to decide they can gain some benefit by backing your social-benefit initiatives.

9. Directly create more demand for the firm's offerings due to the resulting social benefits.

   I believe that foundations can play a role as sources of venture capital, research and resource money, publicity for what you are doing, and sustaining support during lean times. In those roles, foundations can create positive feedback loops that amplify what's good about what you are doing and can attract the interest and support of more people so that their time, energies, and resources can be applied.

Okay, you are probably convinced that you should gain support from foundations. What should you do?

Before approaching foundations, you need to already have clear evidence of the value for how you intend to expand social benefits by 400 times. With that information in hand, you should next research to find all the foundations that have provided any kind of recognition or support for the same or similar benefits. It's from among these foundations that you are most likely to find support. Arrange introductions to such foundations through any credible intermediaries who know you both and ask for the foundations' help in evaluating how appropriate your approach is. In other words, treat them as if they are experts, even if they are not. Take whatever comments you receive seriously and look into what is proposed. If possible, find the answers or tell the foundation staff why it's not practical to do so. Ask for suggestions. Such staffers may well have a solution that you have not thought of. After you have answers, ask for advice on the best way to increase awareness of the information. Chances are pretty good that you'll draw suggestions for what foundations to work with and how to approach them.

If a foundation turns out to be opposed, ask for suggestions to overcome whatever concerns are expressed. The foundation staff may well have a good point that will save much pain and agony. In addition, doing something about the concern will probably lead to your obtaining support from another foundation that will be eager to tell others about the change you made.

After you have quite a few foundations on your side, ask for thoughts about who the most influential critics and opponents are likely to be and what concerns these people may have. Investigate what you can do to deal with these concerns. Then approach these potential opponents to ask for their advice concerning how to improve what you are going to offer. Most people will be flattered to hear from you, knowing that you want to know what can be done better. They will feel as if you are seeing them as experts, even when they are just authoritative foundations.

Take these concerns most seriously. These issues can swamp the boat (or at least your breakthrough solution).

When you think you've covered all the ground you can with foundations and responded appropriately, go public with their observations and support. You'll be glad you did!

What's the key lesson? *An organization that sincerely wants to accelerate its profitable growth can be helped by increasing the current level of social benefits by a much larger (more than 20 times) multiple than the profit increases that it gains from providing the social-benefit expansions in ways that gain support from foundations.*

Your Lesson Seventeen Assignments

1. Identify how gaining support from foundations for your way of increasing social benefits might, in turn, help expand the quantity and types of social benefits provided to attract many more customers and offering and social-benefit end users, and more visible support from them for your organization.

2. Identify how gaining support from foundations for your way of increasing social benefits might help expand purchases from customers who will pay premium prices and provide other economic benefits in support of the social purposes and your organization's ability to profit from this benefit expansion.

3. Evaluate how each social-benefit increase from gaining support from foundations for your way of increasing social benefits could affect each of the nine categories of potential sales and profit increases listed in this and the prior sixteen lessons in terms of attracting and obtaining more support from existing and new stakeholders.

4. Search other industries to find practices that could be brought into your industry to greatly expand the contribution that gaining support from foundations for your way of increasing social benefits makes to the value of your social-benefit increases to customers and current and potential end users for offerings and social benefits.

5. Look beyond what anyone else has done to gain and benefit from support by foundations for your way of increasing social benefits by at least 400 times and company profits by 20 times or more.

Lesson Eighteen

Attract and Involve The General Public

In those days, the multitude being very great and
having nothing to eat, Jesus called
His disciples to Him *and said to them,*
"I have compassion on the multitude, because they have
now continued with Me three days and have nothing to eat.
And if I send them away hungry to their own houses,
they will faint on the way; for some of them have come from afar."

Then His disciples answered Him,
"How can one satisfy these people
with bread here in the wilderness?"

He asked them, "How many loaves do you have?"

And they said, "Seven."

So He commanded the multitude to sit down on the ground.
And He took the seven loaves and gave thanks,
broke them *and gave* them *to His disciples to set before* them;
and they set them *before the multitude.*
They also had a few small fish; and having blessed them,
He said to set them also before them.

So they ate and were filled, and they took up
seven large baskets of leftover fragments.
Now those who had eaten were about four thousand.

And He sent them away,
immediately got into the boat with His disciples,
and came to the region of Dalmanutha.

— Mark 8:1-10 (NKJV)

Mark 8:1-10 (NKJV) shows one way that Jesus attracted more believers. While His words kept large numbers of people spellbound for days, He also knew that they needed real food. Having already fed 5,000 men (plus women and children) on another occasion from a small amount of food that He multiplied, Jesus saw an opportunity to test the faith of His disciples. Not having learned the lesson that Jesus could do anything, they doubted. He decided to give them an object lesson that all things are possible with God. Undoubtedly, seeing the bread and fish miraculously multiplied had a large effect on those who later filled themselves by eating the food. Similarly, greatly increasing social benefits can feel to many people as if a miracle has happened. If you have been faithful in advancing God's Kingdom in so doing, you may, in fact, garner some supernatural support to supplement the wisdom you gain from listening to the Holy Spirit. In any event, the actual provision of the increased social benefits will be powerful evidence to the public that something important is taking place.

With this lesson, we complete our consideration of potential contributors by looking at one final group, people in the general public who are not stakeholders. The purpose of considering them is to focus on attracting large numbers of new stakeholders, something that could not have happened without your exponentially increasing social benefits.

Let me address why I believe that this element is quite important to your sixth complementary 2,000 percent solution by describing various ways that the general public might be attracted. After that, we'll look at how those who are attracted might be involved in socially useful and profitable ways.

First, while many people in the general public don't have any interest in or involvement with your organization, some of them do have strong interests in and involvement with those who will contribute to expanding the social benefits you aim to increase or to those who now or will receive such benefits. When such people appreciate the scale and potential value of what you are trying to do, some will be drawn into being stakeholders and will multiply the effects of what you are doing.

I can cite a personal example to make this point. Prior to learning about the work of the Newman's Own Foundation, I hardly ever bought salad dressing or pasta sauces. I thought of such products as overpriced and too full of calories and preservatives to be part of my diet. After learning how much good the foundation had done in supporting various charities, I began to check out any Newman's Own products I noticed in the supermarket. Today, I rarely make a trip for groceries without buying at least a few of the foundation's healthiest products. I do so for the same reason I usually make a donation to a local charity as I leave the store: I want to share with those in need while I enjoy the bounty of what God has provided for me. Buying the products is a convenient and heart-warming way to do so. So I've become a customer and an end user of Newman's Own. I do this despite there being much less expensive alternatives. I also want to honor the idea of what the foundation is doing so that other organizations will follow this example. As my small contribution, I make special trips to buy coffee at McDonald's because they sell Newman's Own coffee. Do you see how my interests have caused me to become a stakeholder, as well as someone who helps expand profits?

Second, some other people may develop an interest in the social benefits, and such people may ultimately be drawn to your organization if the size and significance of what is provided are great enough. Think of this effect as influencing people to see the world differently through education.

I believe I have used this example before, but let me recycle it (pun intended!). Prior to a few decades ago, there was no financial incentive for customers and end users to recycle beverage bottles and cans. Then, a small fee was added to the price of each container. Whoever returned the bottle or can was refunded the fee. Some people began to make a little extra money by doing this, and the roadsides became cleaner. Today, even though the amount of money involved has become quite small in terms of what it buys in purchasing power, children are fascinated by the idea that they can contribute to improving the environment by recycling these containers. In most households today in the United States, children serve as a sort of environmental police by demanding that family and neighbors recycle such containers. The children become educated through this practice into being concerned about the kind of world that they will live in as adults. With each generation, the commitment by parents and children has grown. Consequently, many people today feel guiltier about not recycling such a container than by inappropriately taking supplies home from work for personal use.

Third, increasing social benefits will cause some members of the general public to come into contact for the first time with beneficiaries or those who provide the benefits ... and to develop an interest in becoming involved in what is being done. Think of this effect as being based on observation and experience. Greatly expanded social benefits will make many people aware for the first time of activities that they would enjoy doing.

As an example, President George H. W. Bush's wife, Barbara, has been a tireless campaigner for increasing the amount of volunteer tutoring done for those who can't read. In doing so, she made many people aware for the first time of how personally rewarding it can be to help an adult or a child with a severe reading problem to become effectively literate. The change seems like a miracle to the learner, and the tutor has the chance to feel like part of the miracle. As a result, the number of volunteers who do such tutoring rapidly increased and remained at higher levels as more people appreciated how desirable this volunteer work is.

Fourth, many people are drawn into activities and changed behavior by someone else. For instance, if your best friend suddenly takes up long-distance bike riding, you'll probably do some investigating into what's involved ... even if you don't decide to participate. With greatly expanded social benefits, the number of people involved in providing and receiving the benefits will enormously increase. All those who are influenced by what these people do will be drawn to make conscious decisions about being involved themselves, many for the first time.

What are the impacts on profits? Let's examine each element on our familiar list once again.

1. Attract more customers and purchases because of customers wanting to support the social purpose.

   Clearly, all four ways of attracting the general public can help here. Through becoming aware of what you do, some members of the general public will become customers or end users for the first time, as I did with Newman's Own.

2. Obtain premium pricing due to the strength of customer desire to support the social purpose or to the marketing benefits received.

   I think the analysis of the four kinds of attraction here is virtually identical to point 1. If your offerings have some demonstrable advantages for customers and stakeholders that the general public cares about, the amount of premium that can be sustained will increase.

3. Reduce costs by receiving volunteer help or reduced charges from suppliers who favor the purpose for the increased social benefits.

   Attracting large numbers of the general public to what you are doing will create a greater percentage increase in these kinds of support, simply because of the effects of social proof (which *Business Basics* discusses for adding customers).

4. Experience fewer costs due to a higher drive among employees, partners, and suppliers for productivity, willingness to work harder in less favorable conditions, and demanding less in payments and benefits.

   To me, the argument is similar to point 3.

5. Avoid investments due to stakeholders doing more of such required investing.

   With substantial public support, governments will be quite cooperative either by providing some of the essential investments or by requiring others to do so.

6. Increase sensitivity to improving cash flow by all stakeholders because of its effect on providing more for those who receive social benefits.

   One of the reasons that Newman's Own is able to support charities so generously is due to lenders being willing to make available all of the investment capital that the organization needs. Similar effects are likely to be true for your organization with greater participation by the general public.

7. Encourage innovative business models that build on the trust and preference for providing and receiving the social benefits.

Most societies are very fragmented in terms of interests and activities. Adding a new major interest opens the door to new ways of operating. Increased interest in soccer playing in the United States has provided a firm foundation for many new ways of facilitating the sport, both at the amateur and professional levels.

8. Potentially receive subsidies from various stakeholders to pay for launching, expanding, or sustaining the benefit provision.

   If direct subsidies are sufficiently powerful to increase social benefits still further, it's feasible to spend the money and time it takes to educate millions of people so that they can decide to provide such subsidies. If there's a tax-saving incentive to do so, such subsidies are even more likely to be increased for those who are interested.

9. Directly create more demand for the firm's offerings due to the resulting social benefits.

   If the social benefits supply great economic advantages, the potential for a rapid increase in demand for offerings is substantial. I think of increasing literacy as an example. When a parent learns to read, the economics of a family are changed forever ... and the government and social costs of supporting the family greatly decline. If providing the social benefits includes mechanisms for capturing some of the value received by beneficiaries, it's very likely that the multiple of social-benefit increases to profit increases for your organization can become still greater.

You are probably convinced now that you should gain support from the general public. How should you go about doing that?

Before appealing to the general public, you need to already have clear evidence of the value of your method for expanding social benefits by 400 times. With that information in hand, you should next research the media habits and activities of those who favor having more of such social benefits available. Concentrate your communications through those media (mostly with public relations) and educational forums connected to these peoples' activities. As new people become involved, encourage them to educate family, friends, and neighbors.

What's the key lesson? *An organization that sincerely wants to accelerate its profitable growth can be helped by increasing the current level of social benefits by a much larger (more than 20 times) multiple than the profit increases that it gains from providing the social-benefit expansions in ways that attract and involve the general public.*

Your Lesson Eighteen Assignments

1. Identify how attracting and involving the general public with your way of increasing social benefits might, in turn, help expand the quantity and types of social benefits provided to attract many more customers and offering and social-benefit end users, and more visible support from them for your organization.

2. Identify how attracting and involving the general public with your way of increasing social benefits might help expand purchases from customers who will pay premium prices and provide other economic benefits in support of the social purposes and your organization's ability to profit from this benefit expansion.

3. Evaluate how each social-benefit increase from attracting and involving the general public with your way of increasing social benefits could affect each of the nine categories of potential sales and profit increases listed in this and the prior seventeen lessons in terms of attracting and obtaining more support from existing and new stakeholders.

4. Search other industries to find practices that could be brought into your industry to greatly expand the contribution that attracting and involving the general public with your way of increasing social benefits make to the value of your social-benefit increases to current and potential customers and end users for offerings and social benefits.

5. Look beyond what anyone else has done to attract and involve the general public with your way of increasing social benefits by more than 400 times and company profits at least 20 times.

Lesson Nineteen

Build a Foundation for An Irresistible Cause

For the word of God is *living and powerful,*
and sharper than any two-edged sword,
piercing even to the division of soul and spirit,
and of joints and marrow, and
is a discerner of the thoughts and intents of the heart.

— Hebrews 4:12 (NKJV)

Hebrews 4:12 (NKJV) reminds us of the power of God's Word, the Bible. When we are tempted to persuade solely with logic, our experiences, and our thoughts, we should remember to first draw on what the Bible says on the subject. Nothing else may be needed to make the right choice.

In the first eighteen lessons, we discuss the potential roles of various stakeholders and groups and how to involve them in the most beneficial ways. Having developed this context for this sixth complementary 2,000 percent solution, it's time to begin to pull together all of these perspectives into a focused strategy and set of plans to implement a solution. As we do so, I want to draw on some metaphors that will probably help focus your thinking more effectively.

As the first of these metaphors, I was tempted to use an irresistible crusade. However, because many people primarily associate the word "crusade" with the times when Christian armies left Europe to attack Muslims in the Middle East, I decided not to use that metaphor. That part of history is not what I have in mind.

Instead, I'm thinking of the sort of community or national commitment to accomplishing some important task that affects virtually everyone in the community or nation. I think of having such a commitment stimulating action as being *an irresistible cause*. To me, the March of Dimes' charitable efforts to find a way to prevent polio were such an irresistible cause.

If you aren't familiar with those efforts, let me tell you a little about them. Polio was infrequently reported until the late 19th century. Yet by the middle of the 1930s, the disease had become quite common and was increasing in frequency. Polio mostly affected children, crippling some and causing others to need artificial assistance to breathe in so-called iron lungs. In many ways, the disease was the most terrifying one of its day, due to whom it affected and how they were affected.

The election of Franklin Delano Roosevelt (FDR) as president of the United States brought a new perspective on the disease. The president had lost the use of his legs from being stricken by the ailment as an adult. Seeing a public health crisis, FDR founded a new charity in 1938, the March of Dimes, for finding a way to protect children from the disease. Everyone in the United States was asked to make a donation of a dime (ten cents) annually towards research and care for polio victims. Within a few years of its founding, the March of Dimes became the best known and most successful charity in the United States and created an improved model for eradicating a disease. The charity's funded research found not one, but two, vaccines that worked. Within 20 years of the organization's inception, the vaccination program was so successful that new cases of the disease all but disappeared.

Let me isolate six elements from that example to consider:

1. The March of Dimes addressed a public problem that was observed almost daily by virtually everyone in the United States and Europe.
2. The problem was one that upset people very much, whether or not they were directly affected.
3. The incidence of polio was a threatening problem that seemed to be destined to become much worse, challenging the very foundations of a healthy society.
4. There was optimism that research could prevent the disease.
5. The victims were most often defenseless children, a group that almost everyone wants to help.
6. There was no apparent contributing fault involved in those who were infected with the crippling disease (unlike, for instance, smokers who contract lung cancer).

Because of these six elements, there was a social consensus that polio must be stopped. I know of no similar social consensus in the United States today. Perhaps the closest that any current issues come to this special status are desires to eliminate illiteracy and autism-spectrum disorders. Awareness, visibility, and concern about these current social problems are, however, much more limited, and they don't receive nearly the same level of focus and attention that the March of Dimes created.

In the very first lesson concerning this complementary source of a sixth 2,000 percent solution, we looked for social benefits that you could improve greatly so that there could be a 400-times improvement. In addition, you were directed to focus on the improvements that would allow you to expand profits by 20 times as you provided these social benefits, through gaining as many advantages as possible from the nine categories of profit benefits that I listed then and that we have been using since to focus our thinking. Since the first lesson, you've been filtering your initial ideas in terms of how your business model and solution might be adapted to work better with stakeholder groups and the general public in ways that would expand social benefits and profits.

As you think about all of the current and potential stakeholder groups we have considered in recent lessons, as well as the general public (our topic in the prior lesson), I'm sure you appreciate that the more emotionally and practically gripped people are by the importance of adding these social benefits, the more cooperation and support will be generated. I want you now to turn your attention to seeing how expanding social benefits can be explained and perceived in ways that will generate the most cooperation and support.

So return to your list of benefits that you focused on during the assignments in Lesson One. We are going to do more work on the fifth assignment: **Consider how motivating providing these social-benefit increases would be to your stakeholders.**

In doing so, I want you to use a template based on the March of Dimes experience to compare to each other the types of social benefits that you could profitably increase:

1. How visible is the lack of these social benefits to your stakeholders and the general public on a daily basis?
2. When people notice that these benefits need to be increased, how upset are they by their lack?
3. How do people perceive the trend and its future implications in terms of any lack of the social benefits you can increase?
4. Do people believe that these social benefits can be greatly increased?
5. How do people feel about those who will be most helped by the increased social benefits?
6. Are those who need the social benefits viewed as not contributing to their need through their own actions and inactions?

As you regard these six elements, be sure to carefully consider both what the perceptions are as well as what the reality is.

After you have done these evaluations for each potential social benefit you might increase, compare what you learn to see if one or more of the potential social benefits you can increase have many more of such elements currently or potentially present.

Next, take the top social-benefit choices and poll your stakeholders and the general public to determine what is actually believed, how belief compares to reality, and what the relative standings are in these terms for the top social-benefits that you might choose to increase.

If you find that perceptions are inaccurate, do a little testing to see how difficult it is to correct any misunderstandings.

Taking these factors into account plus by how much you could increase social benefits, what kind of an impression the increases might make, and what the profit implications probably are, select no more than two social benefits to focus on as a foundation for an irresistible cause. In doing so, feel free to add any other relevant considerations that I haven't listed (such as how difficult it will be to succeed, the consequences of being slow to succeed, and what the costs of flops will be).

What's the key lesson? *An organization that sincerely wants to accelerate its profitable growth can be helped by increasing the current level of social benefits by a much larger (more than 20 times) multiple than the profit increases that it gains from providing the social-benefit expansions in ways that build more of an irresistible cause to succeed among stakeholders and the general public.*

Your Lesson Nineteen Assignments

1. Test how picking one or another of the social benefits you can most profitably increase compares for its potential as a foundation for an irresistible cause as described in the six tests in this lesson. Then put the top choices remaining through this lesson's

assignments 2 through 6 to select no more than two social benefits to emphasize in your breakthrough solution.

2. Identify how picking one or another of the social benefits you can most profitably increase might, in turn, help attract many more customers and offering and social-benefit end users, and more visible support from them for your organization.

3. Identify how picking one or another of the social benefits you can most profitably increase might help expand purchases from customers who will pay premium prices and provide other economic benefits in support of the social purposes and your organization's ability to profit from this benefit expansion.

4. Evaluate how picking one or another of the social benefits you can most profitably increase could affect each of the other categories of potential sales and profit increases listed in the first eighteen lessons in terms of attracting and obtaining more support from existing and new stakeholders.

5. Search other industries to find practices that could be brought into your industry to greatly expand the contribution that picking one or another of the social benefits you can most profitably increase makes.

6. Look beyond what anyone else has done to expand social benefits by at least 400 times and company profits by 20 times or more to identify your top one or two benefits to expand.

Lesson Twenty

Prepare a Path to the Irresistible Cause

Your word is *a lamp to my feet*
And a light to my path.

— Psalm 119:105 (NKJV)

This familiar verse from Psalm 119:105 (NKJV) reminds us that the Bible tells us where we are as well as where we need to go. When this Psalm was written, the Holy Spirit had not yet descended on believers in Jesus. Today, we also have the urgings of the Holy Spirit to attract our attention to the right parts of the Bible and to test our understanding of what to do next. As we do, we can count on the fact that many millions of other believers are being similarly directed, providing the very best source of encouragement for establishing a path to achieving an irresistible cause.

From Lesson Nineteen assignments, you selected no more than two social benefits to expand as the foundation for your irresistible cause. Now, it's time to apply what you learned in answering the Lesson Nineteen assignments to begin changing perceptions in the most positive ways.

As the first step in preparing a path to the irresistible cause, I want you to focus on how to increase the visibility of the lack of these social benefits to your stakeholders and the general public on a day-to-day basis. In working on this task, find ways to inexpensively and ethically draw attention that will be at least as compelling as seeing youngsters cruelly crippled by polio while others were unable to breathe without artificial support from "iron lungs."

In focusing on this opportunity, my suggestion is that you begin by having long, thoughtful conversations with any stakeholders you find who are very aware of the need for more social benefits and feel very strongly about the importance of increasing their availability. My suggestion has two purposes:

1. You may learn better ways to demonstrate the need.
2. You will find out what such stakeholders are most enthusiastic about doing to increase awareness and appreciation of the need.

In many cases, you'll find that these people have had greater contact than you with the consequences of lacking enough social benefits. Some members of their families, or possibly even themselves, may have been personally affected. In many cases, simply relating their own experiences can be a valuable part of expanding awareness for and interest in providing many more social benefits.

A more powerful influence, however, will be to learn about the most affecting connections that they have experienced, especially when such connections can be expanded and made available to other stakeholders as well as ultimately to the general public.

Armed with whatever is learned, I then suggest you contact the most knowledgeable and effective experts concerning the effects of lacking enough social benefits. The experts may add to the list of ways that the effects can be measured, noticed, understood, acted on, and reduced.

Once you have gathered all these sources of information, I next recommend that you draw on the skills of experts in creating awareness and concern about social needs. Share with such experts whatever you have learned about how people gain knowledge that moves them into taking immediate action. See what awareness- and image-improving solutions might be added to what now happens naturally. In considering these solutions, focus on the ones that have the best combination of low cost, not seeming manipulative, and effectiveness in changing awareness, attitudes, and behavior.

Next, systematically approach all the authorities you can who seem like natural allies for increasing awareness of the value of expanding the social benefits by more than 400 times. Explain that you will experiment with ways to add interest and involvement, and ask for their assistance with such efforts.

As the subsequent step, I suggest picking two small geographic areas, one where there's little awareness and interest but there's some reason to think that the potential is high to increase awareness, interest, and activity. The other geographic area should have high awareness and interest, but participation in enhancing the availability of social benefits is low. Then, in each geographic area run a series of tests of the most promising programs you can think of for increasing awareness, interest, and participation.

Then, learn from the tests that work how to design better programs that use more of what is effective and reduce the aspects that are less effective or even harmful. Keep testing.

At whatever point you have reached effectiveness levels that would make the March of Dimes look like a low-profile activity by comparison, you should begin to plan how you can expand the awareness-increasing activities to more geographic areas.

What's the key lesson? *An organization that sincerely wants to accelerate its profitable growth can be helped by increasing the current level of the social benefits by a much larger (more than 20 times) multiple than the profit increases that it gains from providing the social-benefit expansions in ways that build more of an irresistible cause to succeed among stakeholders and the general public by efficiently and effectively increasing awareness of the need for many more social benefits in ways that expand interest, willingness to help, and activity levels.*

Your Lesson Twenty Assignments

1. Take the one or two social benefits you have decided to expand and explore how stakeholders who are very aware of the need to and highly supportive of efforts to increase benefits developed such views. Extract from their experiences lessons that might be applied to other stakeholders, potential stakeholders, and the general public.

2. Contact the most knowledgeable and effective experts concerning the effects of lacking enough of these one or two social benefits. Look for information from the experts that can add to the list of ways that the effects can be measured, noticed, understood, and acted on.

3. Share with experts in creating awareness of and concern about social needs whatever you have learned about how people gain knowledge that moves them into taking immediate action. See what awareness- and image-improving solutions might be added to what happens naturally. In considering these solutions, focus on the ones that have the best combination of low cost, not seeming manipulative, and effectiveness in changing awareness, attitudes, and behavior.

4. Systematically approach all the authorities you can who seem like natural allies for increasing awareness of the value of expanding the social benefits by more than 400 times. Explain that you will experiment with ways to add interest and involvement, and ask for their assistance with such efforts.

5. Pick two small geographies, one where there's little awareness and interest but there's some reason to think that the potential is high to increase awareness, interest, and activity. The other geographic area should be one where awareness and interest are high, but participation in enhancing the availability of social

benefits is low. Then, in each geographic area run a series of tests of the most promising programs you can think of for increasing awareness, interest, and participation.

6. Learn from the tests that work how to design better programs that use more of what is effective and reduce the aspects that are less effective or even harmful. Keep testing.

7. At whatever point you have reached effectiveness levels that would make the March of Dimes look like a low-profile activity in comparison, you should begin to plan how you can expand the awareness-increasing activities to more geographic areas.

Lesson Twenty-One

Polish the Story of Your Irresistible Cause

I will open my mouth in a parable;
I will utter dark sayings of old,
Which we have heard and known,
And our fathers have told us.
We will not hide them *from their children,*
Telling to the generation to come the praises of the LORD,
And His strength and His wonderful works that He has done.

— Psalm 78:2-4 (NKJV)

Jesus loved to teach by using parables, timeless stories that rang true to express lessons all should know and apply about God's Kingdom. He quoted part of Psalm 78:2 (NKJV) in Matthew 13:35 (NKJV) to point out that He was fulfilling prophecy by teaching with parables. We should also tie our stories to accomplishing God's Kingdom purposes. When we do, our stories will ring truer and elicit more support.

In this lesson, we narrow the spotlight to consider just one small aspect of forming new perceptions: polishing the story you will tell about expanding the social benefits being provided by your irresistible cause. As sometimes happens, I received several different clues at the time of this writing that this subject was the right focus for this lesson. Shortly after dawn a female cardinal alit on the windowsill just outside of where I was seated. Almost every time I spot a female cardinal, it's a message that something very important is about to happen. Next, I was working on the last section of Lesson Sixteen of *Excellent Solutions* and decided that it was a good time to remind myself of what I would be covering next in Lesson Seventeen, and the answer was: forming the right story to tell about the excellent solution to gain the most interest and support. After that, I received a call setting up a visit the next day with the former leader of a company where I once worked. As I recalled those years at the company, I remembered how the organization had excelled in turning its knowledge and experiences into motivating stories that captivated people. Then, as I thought about this lesson, I received a strong sense that writing about creating the right story for a cause was critical for turning an ordinary cause into an irresistible one. Finally, I listened to a sermon that night on the subject of how to follow strong intuitive feelings that move your heart. Okay, I surrender, Lord! This lesson is about developing and polishing an irresistible story about your cause. I hope you find it to be useful.

I had also watched a little of the debate that President Obama and Governor Romney conducted the previous night on television in the United States. At one point, Governor Romney attacked by asserting that President Obama had failed to explore for as much oil and gas as possible and demanded that the president confess this weakness. Governor Romney was surprised when President Obama visibly relaxed, smiled, and said something to the effect that Governor Romney had his facts wrong: More drilling was occurring than when President George W. Bush (a Texas oilman) was in office. Subsequent research showed that President Obama was correct. Governor Romney had blundered.

I tell you this example to make a simple point: Even more important than the impact of the story that you craft is its accuracy. If it's not true, or artificially slants things, you will be found out ... and people will run from you and your cause.

Keeping that point about utter truth and accuracy in mind, let's look at how an irresistible story should be crafted and polished.

Building on the homework you did for the previous lesson, I believe that the best possible story will accomplish eight purposes:

1. Make perfectly visible to your stakeholders and the general public any lack in providing these social benefits.
2. Change the emotions of those who hear the story to the most appropriate and sustainable levels of upset and determination to do something about the lack.
3. Establish an accurate perception of the trends that affect the need for the social benefits and their future implications if there should be any deficiency in providing them.
4. Describe an accurate view of what can be done to increase the social benefits.
5. Create appropriate sympathy for those who will be most helped by the increased social benefits.
6. Accurately address any concerns that some may have about some beneficiaries having contributed to their needs through their own actions and inactions.
7. Move the problem from being considered in terms of numbers and statistics to a personal understanding of what providing more social benefits would mean to individuals, families, and communities.
8. Stir the listener or reader to take the most appropriate action.

I recently ran into an example of how such a story might be crafted. Let me share it with you. Imagine that I am developing this story for Habitat for Humanity, the Christian ministry that provides low-cost, single-family homes to poor families in exchange for a down payment of volunteer work by the beneficiaries and paying the rest through retiring an interest-free mortgage. Since the homes are usually built on donated land, with donated materials, and by volunteers, the mortgage may be for as little as one-tenth of the market value of the residence and land. The raw material for my story follows:

> A friend of mine (I'll call her Gloria, not her real name) was away on a trip with her husband. While traveling, Gloria unexpectedly encountered a homeless family. She was deeply distressed to see that one of the youngsters was the same age as one of her own grandchildren ... and had spent the night sleeping on some cardboard under a park bench.
>
> Having shared this information with her friends, one friend immediately advised Gloria to call 911 (the number for emergency services in the United States) and asserted that Social Services would be out quite soon, this family would be put on a short list for housing, and they would probably be housed by nightfall.
>
> Gloria then responded to her friend by noting that she wasn't in the United States. She was in Guatemala. There was nothing to be done through government services.

Can you feel the poignancy of this story? If you are like me, it's a story that you strongly feel in your heart and stomach.

If you are also like me, it gave you a new thought about homelessness. Rather than seeing single people who look like they might be a little sketchy as the homeless, you now see a child being harmed who is a great deal like your own children, nieces, nephews, or grandchildren. You probably started to think about what could be done.

To turn this anecdote into an irresistible-cause story, Habitat for Humanity could have its affiliate in that Guatemalan city contact Gloria and tell her about the programs it has for homeless families with young children. I don't know the details, so I'll just make some up (don't do that, though ... this is just for an illustration of the process!). Let's say that a home could be built for $2,000 (USD) and that it would cost $200 to rent a place for the family to stay until a home could be completed. If the family needed food, that would cost an additional $8 per day. Furniture would be needed, as well. Let's say that the whole budget is $3,500 (USD).

Being big-hearted (and experienced in fund-raising), let's say that Gloria agreed to raise the funds over the next six months. If she could obtain $35 each from 100 people, that would be enough money. While it might be hard to do so in Guatemala, a small church in the United States could easily raise that much.

The family would be helped while the house was built, work on the new home, and eventually move in. Within 10 years, the family would be part of the middle class in Guatemala with a paid-for home worth about $20,000. The $2,000 it had paid in mortgage payments would be used by Habitat for Humanity to cover the costs for providing about 60 percent of a home for another family. Over many decades, several families would be helped by the original donation. Future generations of those families wouldn't be homeless, would gain more education, and would prosper in other ways.

The story could conclude by describing how to raise funds to provide a home for another homeless Guatemalan family with young children.

By the time that the Guatemalan family had been in its new home for about a year, such a story could be constructed based on actual experiences. Or, if someone had already done something like this in Guatemala, Habitat for Humanity could craft a similar story around the prior experience.

Heart-warming experiences could be provided from time to time by Habitat for Humanity by using cell phones to take videos of the beneficiary family and posting them online where the actual donors to this family could see them ... as well as potential supporters of other Guatemalan homeless families.

Does this example give you any ideas? I pray that it does.

As for your process, I encourage you to develop many such stories. Then, test how stakeholders and the general public react to each one so that you can identify ways to improve each story along the lines of the eight purposes I outlined earlier in the lesson. You will probably find that there's no universal story that works best for everyone. By assembling a group of such stories, you'll eventually have ways to tell about your cause that will move almost everyone to take the supporting actions that are needed, much as the March of Dimes drew donations of dimes from almost everyone in the United States, from kindergarteners to people in retirement homes.

What's the key lesson? *An organization that sincerely wants to accelerate its profitable growth can be helped by increasing the current level of the social benefits by a much larger (more than 20 times) multiple than the profit increases that it gains from providing the social-benefit expansions in ways that build more of an irresistible cause to succeed among stakeholders and the general public by crafting and telling accurate, highly appropriate stories to increase awareness of the need for many more social benefits in ways that expand interest, willingness to help, and activity levels.*

Your Lesson Twenty-One Assignments

1. Take what you learned about the one or two social benefits that you will be expanding and develop several true stories that meet the eight purposes for such a story.

2. Test reactions to these stories to identify ways to make each one more effective, while becoming no less truthful.

3. Use the most effective stories to expand awareness of the need for the social benefits and to create interest, willingness to help, and higher activity levels.

Lesson Twenty-Two

Plan an Unmistakable Launch Of Your Irresistible Cause

Now it happened, on a certain day,
that He got into a boat with His disciples.
And He said to them,
"Let us cross over to the other side of the lake."
And they launched out.
But as they sailed He fell asleep.
And a windstorm came down on the lake,
and they were filling with water, *and were in jeopardy.*

And they came to Him and awoke Him, saying,
"Master, Master, we are perishing!"

Then He arose and rebuked the wind and the raging of the water.
And they ceased, and there was a calm.
But He said to them, "Where is your faith?"

And they were afraid, and marveled, saying to one another,
"Who can this be? For He commands
even the winds and water, and they obey Him!"

— Luke 8:22-25 (NKJV)

While the launch of the disciples' boat trip seemed uneventful, I'm sure they never forgot what happened during the crossing. Unless it is God's will, you won't have any miraculous events occurring during the launch of your irresistible cause. Consequently, you'll need to make the launch something that will be hard to mistake or misunderstand for those who are interested in your cause.

Consider the first 2,000 percent solution that we worked on in *Business Basics*, the one for expanding a market by 20 times. You may recall that we considered ways to create one big event that would attract an enormous amount of interest for your type of business offerings. One aspect of that thinking is relevant here: First imagine that you have an unlimited budget for time, money, and effort to gain the most attention for and engagement in your event. Then, take those good ideas and consider how you might accomplish something similar with essentially no time, money, and effort.

Lest you be tempted to simply repeat what you did for that earlier event, let me discourage that approach. This event will work well not due to inherent interest in your type of offering ... but, rather, because of existing and developed interest in providing many more social benefits. Such an event will appeal to much different people and for unrelated reasons.

As we explored while looking at the various stakeholder groups, this shift in appeal is the reason you will be able to access many more experts and celebrities, many of whom will either volunteer their time or will participate in exchange for the opportunity to promote or sell their offerings.

Where the social benefit is important to other organizations, you may be able to access their stakeholders to come to your event. If at least one such organization is a prominent nonprofit, you may be able to access free advertising time and space to promote your activity. If so, an ideal way to do so could be to feature a video or audio version of the introductory stories that we considered how to develop in Lesson Twenty-One.

In addition to advancing the eight purposes you learned about with regard to the stories in the previous lesson, your event should establish a credible commitment to accomplishing your goal of increasing the social benefits by 400 times and describe for all those who are interested what must be done by them and others for this desirable result to occur. To the extent that widely admired, trustworthy people will make statements in support of the goal and the means to get there, you'll have a better platform to speak from in gaining cooperation during the course of everything else you do.

As one way to keep the costs down, I encourage you to think about doing a live Webcast using someone else's Internet connections that can handle substantial video volume. For an organization that already has significant bandwidth, accommodating your need may add little, if any, costs ... especially if you time what you do to occur when the other organization's activities are operating at a relatively low level.

There's other good news. Because of the desirability and appeal of the social benefits you aim to increase, you have the potential to engage a huge audience that would not normally be interested in what your organization does. The added step needed to capture such a potentially larger audience might be as simple as offering a nice prize through a free drawing for those who visit the event and provide contact information for becoming volunteers. In many cases you can even find someone to donate the prize so that all you need are enough volunteers to handle the registrations and drawing on site. If other local businesses might benefit from what you are doing, look into the possibility of their sharing the cost of another crowd-building attraction such as providing a stage for entertainers who volunteer their time or a fireworks show after dark.

If your organization is a global one ... or the social benefits to be expanded will be provided globally, then you should think in terms of either running a series of such events at different times in various locales ... or the potential news value of having one big global event occurring simultaneously in many different venues.

One possible format for such events is the sort of telethon that Jerry Lewis conducted annually for the Muscular Dystrophy Association for about 45 years. During that time, over $2.4 billion dollars were raised in donations from these charity-sponsored telecasts. Raising the money during the telecasts was only part of their value: The programs also taught people about MDA and the needs of those afflicted with muscular dystrophy. The event was staged on or near Labor Day in the United States, a holiday when people often stay home enjoying the last of the summer weather while having a cookout. As a result, television viewership is often quite good that weekend. Because there's not much new competing programming and a charity is involved, my impression is that not much cost was involved in securing the air time. Today, of course, something similar could be done on a low viewership cable television channel and potential access would be quite large at low cost.

As an example of how effective a program like that can be, there's a professional golf association tournament in our area that weekend. Local firemen put out big boots along with signs asking for donations to MDA. Hundreds of thousands of dollars are stuffed into these boots at almost no cost by the tens of thousands of people attending the golf tournament.

I don't mean to dictate what you should do, but, rather, I like to share "success models" of what has worked for others that might get your thinking started. I hope the examples I mentioned have been helpful.

What's the key lesson from this week's topic? *An organization that sincerely wants to accelerate its profitable growth can be helped by increasing the current level of the social benefits by a much larger (more than 20 times) multiple than the profit increases that it gains from providing the social-benefit expansions in ways that build more of an irresistible cause to succeed among stakeholders and the general public by offering a well-planned, unmistakable launch to tell and illustrate highly* *appropriate stories that increase awareness of the need for many more social benefits in ways that expand interest, willingness to help, and activity levels.*

Your Lesson Twenty-Two Assignments

1. Take what you learned about the one or two social benefits that you will be expanding and plan an unmistakable launch event that will powerfully share several true stories that meet the eight purposes for such stories.

2. Test the reactions of your potential participants and stakeholders to identify what features will attract, not discourage, their attendance at such a launch event.

3. Keep developing the plan until you have created a sound platform for meeting the eight purposes.

4. In doing so, carefully consider how you can attract more attention and lower the cost and difficulty of the launch.

Lesson Twenty-Three

Plan Commitment-Building Experiences for Your Irresistible Cause

But this I say*: He who sows sparingly will also reap sparingly,*
and he who sows bountifully will also reap bountifully.
So let *each one* give *as he purposes in his heart,*
not grudgingly or of necessity; for God loves a cheerful giver.
And God is *able to make all grace abound toward you, that you,*
always having all sufficiency in all things,
may have an abundance for every good work.

— 2 Corinthians 9:6-8 (NKJV)

When our hearts are touched, it's only the amount of time, money, and effort available that will limit how much we will commit to helping others. As the Apostle Paul reminds us in 2 Corinthians 9:6-8 (NKJV), God loves for us to be cheerful in providing for others. In this lesson, we consider how to encourage cheerful enthusiasm for the irresistible cause.

Just to review, here's where we are: You have a great story to tell, and you have held a wonderful launch event.

Naturally, you are probably wondering where to go from here. To me the next focus is obvious: Plan commitment-building experiences for your irresistible cause. Let me explain.

If everyone had already developed a deep commitment to expanding these social benefits, there probably wouldn't be much scarcity of such benefits. Since we know that there's a much larger need, there must be a shortage of commitment among the majority of people. Does that make sense?

You might think that almost any kind of experience would work well for increasing commitment. Wrong!

Let me give you some examples involving homeless people, a needy group of particular interest and importance to me. When I see a homeless person, my heart breaks for him or her. From most conversations I have with other people, I get the sense that my reaction isn't unusual.

However, some people judge homeless people as having brought their problems on themselves. Consequently, such people do little to help. Some other people are aware that some homeless people are mentally ill, and these others are afraid to go near. Others are afraid that a homeless person will assault or rob them. Still others are repelled by the inevitable dirt and odors of homelessness.

During a recent discussion I participated in about how to help homeless people, everyone present was glad that there are shelters that provide food and a safe place to sleep. While helpful, shelters don't eliminate the problems.

Some homeless people avoid the shelters. Why?

Well, the shelters are sex-segregated for obvious reasons, and couples would prefer to be together. To enter a shelter, you also have to be reasonably sober. Those who get drunk or "high" at night know they won't be admitted and don't want to give up their substances of choice. Others find the closed-in conditions and noise disturbing. And so on.

Having volunteered at many of Boston's shelters, I know that only one shelter is successful in taking most homeless people and helping them to straighten out their lives, a Christian shelter. The others are operated by nonprofit organizations but get most of their funding from the government, meaning that there's little or no spiritual underpinning to the help. Those places are pretty depressing.

Now, while I could describe dozens of experiences I've had that would convince anyone that they *did not* want to build a personal commitment to helping the homeless, only a few experiences would have, instead, achieved the desired effect of building commitment.

Let me describe a few of the commitment-building experiences. (I'm sure you can figure out on your own what experiences would have the opposite effect.) Here are three such experiences:

1. Perhaps the most powerful experience is seeing someone turn his or her life around, get a job, work hard, and become independent while enjoying a happy life.

   Through my volunteer experiences, I've often had that pleasure. It's a wonderful thing to behold, even if you have played no personal role in it. If you did play a role, it's one of the best feelings in the world.

   Those who are going through such personal rehabilitation often need Christian mentors who meet with them weekly. Taking that role would definitely deepen someone's commitment to helping homeless people.

2. Another powerful experience comes from seeing someone decide to seek rehabilitation. It's often a hard and difficult decision, and homeless people need lots of love and emotional support as they think it through.

   While sharing meals at shelters, many opportunities for such conversations arise. If you visit where homeless people spend daytime hours, you'll also recognize people you know and have fine conversations that will be heart-warming for all of you.

3. I always think of the Parable of the Good Samaritan (from Luke 10) as providing an example. When you see a homeless person in great need, you can stop and provide practical help. It may not be as easy as it sounds. I once saw a homeless man fall on his face and lie helpless. Naturally, I wanted to help him up. It took all my strength to do so, and that wasn't enough until he started pushing a bit, as well.

   While you won't necessarily see an opportunity like this one, you'll find one often enough to encourage you to keep your eyes open for ways to help.

The key point I would like to make is that due to such experiences most people would no longer find any contact with a homeless person to be anything other than a possible source of joy. I won't go further into the examples because I trust you to take me at my word.

With regard to your irresistible crusade, you have a parallel challenge to accomplish two tasks:

1. Find the experiences that build commitment to the cause in almost anyone.
2. Plan ways that such experiences can be easily accessed and seem more appealing to those who are skeptical about the cause.

A good place to start is by speaking to those who are already most committed to the cause to find out what, if any, experiences contributed to their level of commitment. Ask for their advice, as well, concerning whether and how others should be introduced to the same, similar, or different experiences. As an example, I've found that most people are quite willing to do volunteer work with homeless people if someone first describes what's involved and then accompanies the volunteer for the initial occasions.

It's also good to ask the beneficiaries how they think that people become more committed to helping them. Chances are that they have heard such stories on many occasions.

From there, I suggest imagining ways to combine experiences to enhance the effects and make increasing commitment easier and more efficient to accomplish.

Ultimately, you need to run tests, learn from them, revise what you do, and keep learning. Once you know what you want to do, online videos of such experiences are a great way to encourage interest and understanding. Also, find people who will film either reality television shows or documentaries that advocate the experiences.

Finally, be sure that the ensuing experiences are so powerful that those who have them will tell poignant stories to everyone they meet.

What's the key lesson? *An organization that sincerely wants to accelerate its profitable growth can be helped by increasing the current level of the social benefits by a much larger (more than 20 times) multiple than the profit increases that it gains from providing the social-benefit expansions in ways that build more of an irresistible cause to succeed among stakeholders and the general public by encouraging and providing commitment-building experiences that increase awareness of the need for many more social benefits in ways that expand interest, willingness to help, and activity levels.*

Your Lesson Twenty-Three Assignments

1. Determine what experiences have built the most commitment for your irresistible cause.

2. Test reactions to various ways of providing such experiences.

3. Find ways to combine experiences that intensify the effects and make them longer lasting.

4. In doing so, consider how you can attract more attention and lower the cost and difficulty of providing the experiences.

5. Look for ways to overcome any concerns about engaging in such experiences.

Lesson Twenty-Four

Attract Large Numbers of People to Commitment-Building Experiences

Now after six days Jesus took Peter, James, and John, and
led them up on a high mountain apart by themselves;
and He was transfigured before them.
His clothes became shining, exceedingly white, like snow,
such as no launderer on earth can whiten them.
And Elijah appeared to them with Moses,
and they were talking with Jesus.
Then Peter answered and said to Jesus,
"Rabbi, it is good for us to be here;
and let us make three tabernacles:
one for You, one for Moses, and one for Elijah"
— because he did not know what to say,
for they were greatly afraid.
And a cloud came and overshadowed them;
and a voice came out of the cloud, saying,
"This is My beloved Son. Hear Him!"
Suddenly, when they had looked around,
they saw no one anymore, but only Jesus with themselves.

— Mark 9:2-8 (NKJV)

To develop three of His disciples, Jesus took Peter, James, and John to a high mountain where He was transfigured, Elijah and Moses appeared, and a voice came out of a cloud proclaiming Jesus as His Son. If you are like me, such an event would definitely have caught your attention and dispelled any doubts about committing to whatever Jesus asked of you. While it would be wonderful if such an intense, unique supernatural experience could be recreated to increase commitment by large numbers of people, that's not likely to happen. In this lesson, we look at how to improve commitment by providing valuable experiences that many people can and will want to engage in.

The previous lesson ended with this charge: Be sure that the ensuing experiences are so powerful that those who have them will tell poignant stories to everyone they meet. Keeping that perspective in mind, the next task is to take such experiences and attract large numbers of people to engage in and be transformed by them. In doing so, you may find some of the following issues:

1. In the current form, such experiences could only be provided to a small number of people.

2. Despite having made the experiences seem, in advance, to be more appealing, most people would still rather take a vacation in a garbage dump than participate in your most interesting-sounding, commitment-building experience.

3. There's no easy way to make the commitment-building experiences available to more people or to seem more appealing in advance.

By engaging stakeholders and the general public in some of the commitment-building experiences, you'll have their experiences and reactions as resources to help you overcome some aspects of these limitations. Here are examples of what you can learn by interviewing those who have completed the experiences:

1. What you said or did that led them to decide to engage in the experiences.

2. What you said or did that caused the most reluctance.

3. What others said to them who decided not to engage.

4. What those who had the experiences believe would be better ways to attract interest and participation.

5. Recommendations for "mini" experiences that would probably serve almost as effectively as the "full" experience that they had.

6. Improved ways of describing what the experiences involve.

7. Revisions in the experiences that would make them sound and be more appealing.

You will probably find that some small percentage of those who engage in the experiences will be tremendously energized and encouraged by doing them. In fact, some of these people may want to be involved every day in doing this work. Find ways to engage them. Their enthusiasm will make the experiences more powerful and effective for everyone else.

Many people are also attracted to doing things because it's a step toward something that they have an enormous desire to do. Consider all the difficult training that potential astronauts go through without ever knowing if they will actually lift off the Earth in a rocket. Those who return from space report that their lives are never the same. Those who made it to the moon reported even greater changes in perception.

While focusing on experiences that connect to what people have an enormous desire to do, I suggest that you then look into developing a sequence of experiences ... each one of which is more exciting and engaging than the previous ones. Use awareness of these opportunities to attract people into doing the entry-level experiences.

If no other possibilities exist, consider having celebrity participants in these more advanced activities that will generate publicity for the cause. Perhaps each person could have a photo opportunity with the celebrity or celebrities with the resulting image also being offered to local news outlets.

You can also tie in more advanced commitment-building experiences to rewarding those who have done the most to support your activity. As an example, my wife and I were sponsors of the Boston Symphony Orchestra for many years. One year we were invited for a several-hour experience of what it's like to be a member of the orchestra. One of the high points of the experience was sitting in the orchestra's seats on stage while thousands of balloons were released, as happened at the end of some Boston Pops concerts. I'll never forget it!

I also suggest that you look into the effectiveness of various ways to capture the commitment-building experiences for others to appreciate. For instance, you might interview those who are having the experiences at the most appealing points and make videos of what they said available to those who are considering the experience opportunity. You could also encourage those engaged in the activity to send e-mails and postcards to friends and family that provide an easy way for the person contacted to arrange to have the same experience. If there are any beneficiaries involved, be sure that they have opportunities to explain what it means to them to have people becoming more engaged with them.

Ultimately, if you are going to expand from a few dozen people at a time having a high-quality experience to thousands of people doing so, you will probably find it attractive to create interactive virtual experiences that involve access to those engaged in providing and receiving the social benefits. With today's technology, such experiences can be both high quality and inexpensive. By eliminating the need for people to travel to specific locations and to fit into certain spaces, you also expand how many people can participate.

Such activities can also be combined with more hands-on experiences. For instance, such a virtual experience might be provided at a local venue at which a few beneficiaries and benefit providers speak briefly, with opportunities to converse with them afterward.

Don't assume that everyone should have the same experiences. Retain some hands-on, small-group activities, as well as offering individualized experiences that can be conducted remotely.

Perhaps the most important point is to track those who have different kinds of experiences to see if what is provided has any influence on how much action they take and how effectively in supporting the irresistible cause. Let the results of such measurements ultimately guide the development of how you attract many more people and provide commitment-building experiences for them.

What's the key lesson? *An organization that sincerely wants to accelerate its profitable growth can be helped by increasing the current level of the social benefits by a much larger (more than 20 times) multiple than the profit increases that it gains from providing the social-benefit expansions in ways that build more of an irresistible cause to succeed among stakeholders and the general public by attracting large numbers of people to commitment-building experiences that increase awareness of the need for many more social benefits in ways that expand interest, willingness to help, and activity levels.*

Your Lesson Twenty-Four Assignments

1. Test ways to make the experiences you offer more effective in increasing cause-supporting activities.

2. Investigate ways to expand the activities so more people can participate.

3. Look for ways to create follow-on activities that will increase interest in participating in entry-level activities.

4. Explore ways to use "high-tech, high-touch" solutions to increase participation without increasing costs or diluting the impact on those who participate.

5. Find ways to gain more attention for the experiences that people have in these activities.

6. Continually measure and study how the nature of the experiences received affects the level and type of actions taken to support the public cause.

Lesson Twenty-Five

Train People to Perform Key Tasks

"A disciple is not above his teacher, but everyone who is perfectly trained will be like his teacher."

— Luke 6:40 (NKJV)

Luke 6:40 (NKJV) teaches us three important truths. First, disciples will be like their teachers. Second, only with perfect training will disciples be exactly like their teachers. Third, perfect training means that any flaws in the teachers will be evident in the disciples. We need to keep these truths in mind as we consider how to turn the swell of commitment to the irresistible cause into fruitfulness for the Lord's purposes.

Our attention shifts in this lesson to training people to perform key tasks for the irresistible cause. As you can imagine, developing the stories, communicating them, and engaging large numbers of people in commitment building will eventually pave the way for some people to want to learn the key tasks required by an irresistible cause, whether in serving as volunteers or as employees.

If you have made your preparations well, you might go rather quickly from having just a few people trained to having quite a large number of people wanting to be trained. As you can imagine from that description, you would then need to place a high priority on first training people who can be trainers of other trainers.

Naturally, if someone has already been successful in preparing trainers, that success is a good indication of the person's potential to play a similar role for your irresistible cause. But who else can be helpful?

I believe that experts and authorities can also be a big help by making those who want to be trained feel that they are being offered something quite special and more valuable. After you have attracted experts and authorities, a good next step is to design the training to make the best use of the availability of these experts. For instance, the most dedicated people who want to train trainers may also be motivated by chances to mix and mingle with experts and authorities. In so doing, the future trainers of trainers will also gain stories, experiences, and credibility that will be useful when they are training others to be trainers. As a result, make it easy for trainers to rub shoulders with much-admired role models.

With such interesting opportunities, who else should be sought to become trained to train others? Well, those who already do effective adult teaching are good prospects. Two frequently overlooked sources for such people are those who teach adult-education classes and tutor in subjects that are at least somewhat related to the kind of training to be done.

You might be wondering why I don't suggest school teachers as the top of the list of candidates to seek. Well, these hard-working people often have little spare time during the school year. Some of them arrange for regular seasonal employment over summer recesses. But if you operate in places where school teachers may well have time and interest in training trainers, by all means seek them out.

University professors are often contractually limited in how much time they can devote to matters unrelated their schools' activities. In many cases, they are also more helpful in sharing knowledge of research findings than in providing top teaching skills.

One advantage of training people who already train others is that they are usually quick learners and can succeed, even if the material they receive isn't as well developed as it will eventually be. By using whatever materials are available, they become an excellent source of insights for how those materials and the initial learning process can be improved.

I further suggest that thought be given to how videos and self-paced online learning can be used to permit as much of the trainer training to occur without needing a vast army of trainers. Such methods might be able to reduce the lag in starting up by many months, and possibly even years.

Likewise, some thought should go into what opportunities exist to provide hands-on training in apprenticeship-style learning programs, enabling those who are doing the training to focus on demonstrating what is to be done differently (if at all) from what people who do that and similar tasks already know how to do. To facilitate such training, it can be useful to have curriculum developers for training programs work with those who have related task expertise and training experience to determine what new materials, if any, are required to direct whatever training is actually required. In doing so, consider how Habitat for Humanity organizes its building projects to accomplish almost everything using volunteers who have relatively little, if any, building experience and skill to draw on.

In addition, consider if any tasks can be reorganized so that fewer and simpler-to-learn skills are required. If so, the need for trainers of trainers can be substantially decreased.

Further, look into ways that automation might reduce either the required training by simplifying what needs to be done or through eliminating the potential for errors that require a lot of training in how to avoid and overcome. In some cases, such automation can reduce training time by more than 98 percent. Such automation has been critical in helping fast-food chains, for example, deal with their perpetual shortages of people who can take orders and correctly operate electronic cash registers. In many cases, order takers need only look for photos of the products that are being ordered and then push the corresponding buttons.

Finally, consider how those who are being trained could also receive enough information so that they could be quickly converted into trainers, even if they have little experience and knowledge in the area or in training. For instance, during World War II newly minted American pilots who scored well in flight-training programs for fighter pilots were often assigned to immediately provide training to brand-new pilots.

What's the key lesson? *An organization that sincerely wants to accelerate its profitable growth can be helped by increasing the current level of the social benefits by a much larger (more than 20 times) multiple than the profit increases that it gains from providing the social-benefit expansions in ways that succeed in building an irresistible cause faster among stakeholders and the general public by quickly training enough people to perform key tasks.*

Your Lesson Twenty-Five Assignments

1. Identify ways you can rapidly build a corps of trainers who can train other trainers.

2. Consider ways to make it more appealing and interesting to develop such skills.

3. Consider how any training might be supplemented or replaced by apprenticeship-style programs.

4. Further test how tasks can be simplified to reduce training.

5. Investigate opportunities to use automation to eliminate training requirements.

6. Explore ways that newly trained people could be immediately turned into effective trainers.

Lesson Twenty-Six

Create a Foundation for Replacing a Government Activity

Let every soul be subject to the governing authorities.
For there is no authority except from God, and
the authorities that exist are appointed by God.
Therefore whoever resists the authority
resists the ordinance of God,
and those who resist will bring judgment on themselves.

For rulers are not a terror to good works, but to evil.
Do you want to be unafraid of the authority?
Do what is good, and you will have praise from the same.
For he is God's minister to you for good.

— Romans 13:1-4 (NKJV)

The Apostle Paul exhorts us in Romans 13:1-4 (NKJV) to combine with government authorities to accomplish good. Whenever I read about how some Christians focus their energies on opposing their governments, I wonder if such believers have read these verses. In this lesson, we'll explore a new way to combine forces with governments to accomplish God's good purposes.

In the previous seven lessons, we pulled together all of the perspectives from the initial eighteen lessons for engaging stakeholders and the general public with developing a breakthrough solution, a focused strategy, and a set of plans for implementing the solution in terms of the metaphor of establishing an irresistible cause. Now, we begin looking at second kind of breakthrough solution, a related strategy, and a set of plans for implementing this solution: replacing a government activity. This lesson provides the foundation for developing this second approach.

In most cases where social benefits are involved, you will probably find that there are existing government programs ranging from cash being distributed to (or taxes reduced for) beneficiaries to direct assistance being supplied through government employees (such as social workers) or contractors (such as distributors of surplus food). Since these government programs aren't often based on 2,000 percent solution principles and methods, it's likely that redirecting whatever the programs now cost to being used to fund the breakthrough solution will be more than sufficient to launch and sustain the new activity in supplying many more benefits.

Naturally, anyone using such an approach can expect to be opposed by those who have an interest in sustaining what is being done now. Here are some of the likely opponents you should expect:

- Government workers who will lose jobs or benefits that they like
- Government contractors who will lose profitable business
- Unions that represent either government workers or those who work for contractors
- Those who originally designed the programs
- Politicians who gain benefits from having supported or by supporting the existing programs

- Beneficiaries who fear that their interests will be harmed by any changes
- Advocacy groups that philosophically favor different methods for providing benefits
- Candidates for public office who believe that many people fear or oppose the breakthrough solution
- Academics whose research favors alternative approaches
- Skeptics of committing resources to something new
- Competing developers of new methods that they would like to substitute for the existing government programs

Well, with so much potential resistance, how can anyone hope to gain approval for substituting the breakthrough solution for the existing government programs? In practice, rapid substitution isn't likely to occur. However, given the scale of the resources that are potentially available, obtaining even a modest amount of such resources can be a huge windfall. Consider that if benefits will, in fact, be increased by 400 times, then the breakthrough solution needs only to gain one-quarter of 1 percent of the current resources being applied to match the output of the existing program.

Can you imagine the ability to draw favorable attention to a circumstance where using 0.25 percent of the resources exceeds the benefits generated by 99.75 percent of the resources? Naturally, the consensus of what should be done would shift pretty quickly.

There's another point: Any resistance will have significant power only in circumstances where the government is oversupplying what beneficiaries actually need and want in ways that are satisfying and the government has no need to operate more efficiently because of having more than enough financial resources. In today's world, it's a rare country and an even rarer benefit provision that can draw on these kinds of favorable conditions as reasons to maintain the status quo.

Naturally, you don't have to initially attract the attention of every government. You can begin by just focusing on the ones that are in the most desperate straits in terms of providing much needed benefits and being able to pay for doing so. From such hard-up government entities, you'll find more than enough interest to allow you to perform demonstration projects.

As you seek to obtain such opportunities, I strongly urge you to keep in mind where demonstration projects would be most persuasive for those governments under less pressure to increase benefits and reduce the costs of providing them. One way to do so is by looking at what other governments have copied innovations that an individual government has done in the past. Another way to gain such insights is by speaking to those who run government benefit programs to find out how they would evaluate the kinds of demonstration projects that you might engage in to assist various governments. Take the time to seek the advice of academics and authorities about what issues they would like to see tested in demonstration projects so that such individuals are more likely to advance your cause after a demonstration project succeeds.

As you seek such opportunities, be sure to obtain agreement on what performance would have to occur before those involved would join you in seeking to substitute the breakthrough solution for some or all of the government programs. Doing so will help draw more attention to your demonstration and also reduce the delay in going from a demonstration to a fuller implementation.

Some skittish governments may not want to take any chances on what you offer and will only allow you to run demonstration projects if you pay all the costs. If you can afford to do so and the economic benefits are substantial enough, go ahead. Chances are that option won't be your preferred choice. In such instances, I encourage you to ask foundations and grant-providing organizations to fund any such demonstrations. Such funding is popular now, especially where the potential benefit increases are quite high and there is ultimately no need to add resources.

Another potential approach is to explore ways that providing more benefits can become self-funding. Consider food stamps in the

United States, a relatively expensive part of supporting families and individuals who lack sufficient income to meet their needs. If one benefit of your breakthrough solution is that incomes of such beneficiaries will rise so much that food stamps can be eliminated, you might seek to obtain an agreement with the government agency that reduces costs from such a shift to share some of the savings with your organization. While such an approach might cause you to still incur substantial costs and investments in the short-term, the agreement might permit you to turn a profit on highly successful demonstration projects in the long term and set a precedent for a later agreement when a larger-scale replacement of government activity occurs. In making this comment, I'm reminded of the contracts that H. Ross Perot successfully negotiated with governments many decades ago while heading Electronic Data Systems that provided for generous sharing of any cost reductions his firm generated.

While unlikely, the self-funding source might come from outside the government. For instance, if your benefit provision is to help low-income people gain jobs at which they are very productive, you might be able to charge a conditional fee to the employers who decide to keep the newly prepared employees after an appropriate training and probationary period.

Don't be limited to just my ideas. Explore any sources of demonstration project funding that make sense in terms of your breakthrough solution.

What's the key lesson? *An organization that sincerely wants to accelerate its profitable growth can be helped by increasing the current level of the social benefits by a much larger (more than 20 times) multiple than the profit increases that it gains from providing the social-benefit expansions in ways that replace a government activity.*

Your Lesson Twenty-Six Assignments

1. Identify who will oppose your breakthrough solution replacing existing government activities.

2. Consider ways to reduce such opposition.

3. Look for governments that are less likely to be influenced by such opposition.

4. Explore how the results of demonstration projects for such governments can have greater influence on decision makers in other governments.

5. Consider how the cost of demonstration projects can be reduced through approaches such as by obtaining grants, gaining payments for reduced costs from governments, and charging fees to third parties based on results.

6. Develop a demonstration-project process that will attract positive comments and interest whenever any such project succeeds in outperforming the existing methods.

Lesson Twenty-Seven

Replace a Government Activity by Gaining Financing for Beneficiaries

When you reap your harvest in your field,
and forget a sheaf in the field,
you shall not go back to get it;
it shall be for the stranger, the fatherless, and the widow,
that the LORD your God may bless you
in all the work of your hands.
When you beat your olive trees,
you shall not go over the boughs again;
it shall be for the stranger, the fatherless, and the widow.
When you gather the grapes of your vineyard,
you shall not glean it *afterward;*
it shall be for the stranger, the fatherless, and the widow.

— Deuteronomy 24:19-21 (NKJV)

In Deuteronomy 24:19-21 (NKJV), Moses told the Israelites what God had said to him. In this portion of that chapter, God described a way that those with an agricultural surplus could painlessly provide for those who lacked, who were most often strangers, fatherless children, and widows. Notice that those who needed help had to work to get it. But the provision was there for the energetic. Similarly, some people just need a financial stake to get them started in solving their problems. In this lesson, we look at ways governments today might provide funds to beneficiaries that could be used to pay for receiving greatly expanded social benefits.

In Lesson Twenty-Six, we considered ways to establish successful demonstration projects and to gain enough support to offset the expected opposition to replacing a government activity. Those observations will certainly apply no matter how you choose to replace a government activity.

Another approach for replacing a government activity has often worked well in the United States: offering an economic incentive to beneficiaries to switch from the government alternative. While I have no idea how well the approach would work in your country, it's certainly worth taking a little time to think about it.

Let me share an example to make the concept easier to understand. In the United States, almost everyone over the age of 65 is eligible for some form of highly subsidized health insurance that is underwritten by the national government. The most common form is called Medicare.

For many years, the federal government was also the only administrator of this program. So if you wanted Medicare, you asked for it and paid whatever was charged.

Private companies saw this provision as a potential source of profit. In many cases, private health insurers were doing so much business with doctors and hospitals in the geographic areas that they served that these insurers had succeeded in negotiating very low rates. If such companies could also add Medicare patients, they would be able to negotiate even lower rates. Even if little or nothing was earned on the Medicare business, the cost reductions for servicing the other patients would greatly add to profits on that part of the business. Eventually, the government authorized such organizations to provide Medicare alternatives that were subsidized to the same extent by the taxpayers. Let me explain how that came about and what its implications were.

As you can imagine, such an expensive program creates a lot of political controversy. Taxpayers would like to see it cost less. They often advocate cutting benefits offered. Those who are gaining the benefits would like even more coverage ... and they would like to pay less. Since there are more people paying taxes than those who are on Medicare, the size of benefits looked like it was in jeopardy.

These private companies were able to argue that they would provide more coverage ... at less cost, just what people who are on Medicare wanted. At the same time, such cost containment somewhat mollified the taxpayers due to the potential that the rate of cost increases for the program might be reduced.

So the federal government authorized some experiments, and such private insurers did very well. Those who chose insurance coverage from the private insurers probably did even better. And taxpayers had no reason to be grumpy.

If you were to duplicate this strategy, you might have to seek new legislation or changes in regulations that would permit you to offer a service or product alternative to what the government or its monopoly supplier does. Naturally, a monopoly supplier isn't going to be very interested in allowing that change. Government workers who might lose their jobs aren't going to be thrilled either.

To break the deadlock, you should do your homework and then offer an economic incentive to the customers or beneficiaries of your service or product that will lead them to bang loudly on the doors of the appropriate government officials demanding to get something better from you. That reaction is most likely to occur where the government provision is inadequate in quality or insufficient in supply. I believe that offering cleaner water in urban areas at low cost where it's hard to obtain from a government monopoly could be such an opportunity.

To avoid the potential conflict with government employees who fear layoffs, I suggest your initial proposal be to offer a level of service or products that may divert some of the growth in consumption but will leave plenty of activity for the government employees to do. If you absorb most of the growth over time, your activity will eventually supersede what the government does, but without being threatening to those who are worried about their jobs.

Another approach to overcoming government control can be found in American education. To encourage more people to attend college and graduate school, the U.S. government offers a generous program of guaranteed student loans. Because the loans are backed by the full faith and credit of the United States, the borrowing cost is low. Students who wouldn't be able to borrow on their own credit can obtain these loans.

Traditionally, such loans were used mostly for attending community and state colleges and universities, the least expensive places to seek a degree. For-profit colleges and universities appreciated that there could be a profitable opportunity for them: Take students who couldn't get into public colleges and universities and have them pay with student loans. In essence, the government was indirectly financing the growth of these private institutions. Such for-profit schools lobbied for the government to greatly increase the loan limits, and the rest is history.

Your industry may need some financing push like that of such subsidized loans so that those who need the benefits you want to provide can afford to purchase until receiving enough of the benefits increases their incomes or buying power. If there's a general public benefit involved and many individuals would be helped, you will find allies in encouraging the government to provide such financing. In times when employment is depressed, there will be pressure on the government to redirect people into education as one way to reduce the unemployment rate in the near term and to increase the long-term employment rate by preparing more effective workers.

A third American example also comes from education, this time in elementary and secondary schools. For many years, low-income students in urban schools performed poorly. Yet the expenditures per student were quite large. Clearly, there was an effectiveness issue here.

Private companies also spotted this problem as a profit opportunity and opened schools. In doing so, the companies sought financing from the local school districts to pay for their students who come from the public schools that were poorly performing. If such schools can improve student outcomes, students flock to them. If they can do so at a low cost, they earn a handsome profit. Social benefits are obviously much larger in this case. In essence, these students are having their tuition and book costs covered by the government through the local school district.

Although public-school teachers and their unions are very nervous about these for-profit schools, they don't have enough political strength to fight such a change.

I don't know if any of these examples inspires any ideas for your country, but I certainly hope so. Please share your ideas with me. I'll look forward to hearing from you.

What's the key lesson? *An organization that sincerely wants to accelerate its profitable growth can be helped by increasing the current level of the social benefits by a much larger (more than 20 times) multiple than the profit increases that it gains from providing the social-benefit expansions in ways that replace a government activity through gaining financing for beneficiaries.*

Your Lesson Twenty-Seven Assignments

1. Identify places where existing government activities are being criticized, need to become more efficient, or are in short supply.

2. Consider more efficient ways to accomplish such activities.

3. Determine who will be opposed to making a change in favor of private enterprise.

4. Explore methods for providing an alternative that will not be overly threatening to those who will be opposed.

5. Develop a financing plan that will provide beneficiaries and taxpayers with reasons for hope.

6. Find potential allies who might favor such an approach and explain how they will benefit.

7. Develop a superior track record in providing an alternative.

8. Gradually become the dominant provider by doing a better job at lower cost while growing through just taking most of the expansion in benefit provision, so others don't lose their jobs.

Lesson Twenty-Eight

Replace a Government Activity with Private Financing for Beneficiaries

There were also some *who said,*
"We have mortgaged our lands and vineyards and houses,
that we might buy grain because of the famine."

There were also those who said,
"We have borrowed money for the king's tax
on *our lands and vineyards.*
Yet now our flesh is *as the flesh of our brethren,*
our children as their children; and indeed
we are forcing our sons and our daughters to be slaves,
and some *of our daughters have been brought into slavery.*
It is *not in our power* to redeem them,
for other men have our lands and vineyards."

– Nehemiah 5:3-5 (NKJV)

Nehemiah 5:3-5 (NKJV) shows how debt can be terrible for poor people. To advance God's purposes using private financing, we need to ensure that such harm will not occur.

Lesson Twenty-Seven builds on the prior lesson's foundation by looking at how to obtain financing for beneficiaries to make the government-replacement activity available. In that lesson, we concentrate on gaining the necessary funds from governments. In this lesson, we look at the same opportunity to replace a government activity, except this time by relying on private financing.

Let me give you some examples that may trigger innovative thinking. We'll start with launching new enterprises. Traditionally the governments in sub-Saharan Africa have spent enormous sums received from more developed nations to train, equip, and encourage new business leaders. Most such efforts don't bear much fruit. The training and loans are received by people who want to start businesses, the funds are spent on something, the businesses eventually collapse, the loans are not repaid, and the businesspeople start looking for new loans to start another business. Those who work with such programs report that free money can be addictive, rather than helpful, for entrepreneurs.

A student of mine in Malawi, Donald Kamdonyo, Ph.D., undertook to see what could be done to help entrepreneurs in other ways. He invested a little of his own money to rent a place to hold classes about entrepreneurship for leaders of marginal small businesses. By working closely with his students, he learned that they lacked some basic disciplines needed to succeed, such as keeping personal and business funds separate, filling out the required paperwork to qualify for supplying government contracts, showing up for work on time, and paying their bills when due. He developed a course module to teach the importance of these practices and to provide practical training in how to do them properly.

Once these habits were instilled, the small businesses started to do much better. Still, many of them were operating on too little capital. Because they lacked good credit, they could not borrow to expand their businesses.

At that point, Donald began to teach lessons for applying 2,000 percent solution methods to expand sales by 20 times, reduce costs by 96 percent, and eliminate 96 percent of all investment needs. In several cases, the small businesspeople had opportunities to become government suppliers. After obtaining such contracts, they learned ways to find financing from suppliers to tide them over until such time as the government payment was made. In these activities, such entrepreneurs often began supplying goods and services that had formerly been provided by government employees. Unlike in many Western countries where government contracts are typically low-margin opportunities, Donald found that the resulting profit margins were generous for low bidders. With such financing in place, these entrepreneurs were able to then bid for large private contracts and supply them, too, at high profit margins. So such private financing allowed his beneficiaries to help themselves to rapidly expand their incomes, their hiring, and their net worths. If you would like to learn more about Donald's work and the use of such private financing, I highly recommend his book, *Poverty by Choice: Why Some People Are Wallowing in Poverty and How They Can Earn Their Share of the World's Wealth* (2013).

Financing of inventory, equipment, and high quality receivables is often done by businesses in most countries. If providing the public benefit in replacing a government activity requires having inventory and equipment, and high-quality receivables are generated, then private financing will be readily available. Most governments are on a cash basis for accounting purposes. Consequently, expanding some programs that they want to do which require more capital than the annual budget can bear may require nothing more than leasing some equipment and financing some inventory. The government receivable is generally considered to be high quality and can be turned into financing for doing such work on the government's behalf. If your beneficiaries can be hired to do some of this work while serving other beneficiaries, you'll help expand benefits even faster.

In many nations, there's an activity for providing housing to at least some of the poorest people who have other disadvantages, such as physical disabilities. Such housing is often poorly maintained, and is often located in a crime-infested neighborhood. Yet, a Christian charity, Habitat for Humanity, often goes into the very same neighborhoods and builds sturdy, low-cost individual homes (with volunteers and donations of land, materials, and skilled labor) that beneficiary families purchase through a combination of sweat equity earned by working on the building and acquiring a no-interest mortgage from Habitat for Humanity. I don't know that anyone from Habitat has ever looked into replacing such government housing projects, but if Habitat doesn't already do so, a new enterprise certainly could. With today's interest rates quite low in many countries around the world, part of the financing could be provided by conventional first mortgage loans for a smaller-than-usual portion of the home's value. By being more efficient, such a builder could probably afford to subsidize a second mortgage to cover the rest of the price at a level of monthly payments that could be afforded by a low-income family that couldn't qualify for a Habitat house.

What's the key lesson? *An organization that sincerely wants to accelerate its profitable growth can be helped by increasing the current level of the social benefits by a much larger (more than 20 times) multiple than the profit increases that it gains from providing the social-benefit expansions in ways that replace a government activity through gaining private financing for beneficiaries.*

Your Lesson Twenty-Eight Assignments

1. Identify places where existing government activities are being criticized, need to become more efficient, or are in short supply.

2. Consider more efficient ways to accomplish such activities.

3. Determine who will be opposed to making a change in favor of private enterprise.

4. Explore methods for providing an alternative that will not be overly threatening to those who will be opposed.

5. Develop a private financing plan that will provide beneficiaries and taxpayers with reasons for hope.

6. Find allies who will favor such an approach and explain to them how they will benefit.

7. Develop a superior track record in providing an alternative.

8. Gradually become the dominant provider by doing a better job at lower cost while growing through just taking most of the expansion in benefit provision so others don't lose their jobs.

Lesson Twenty-Nine

Replace a Government Activity by Directly Financing Beneficiaries

I have been young, and now *am old;*
Yet I have not seen the righteous forsaken,
Nor his descendants begging bread.
He is *ever merciful, and lends;*
And his descendants are *blessed.*

— Psalm 37:25-26 (NKJV)

The Bible is rightly cautious about encouraging borrowing and lending, except to assist those in need. For such a purpose, the Israelites were prohibited from charging interest on their loans. In today's world, the neediest often pay, instead, the highest rates of interest, if they can even find anyone to lend to them. Lending that seeks to expand God's Kingdom is a different story, however, one that this lesson explores.

Our subject is how it might be attractive to directly finance some or all of the beneficiaries, rather than seeking public or traditional, private financing sources. I see such opportunities existing primarily when government and private sources would probably not be available, while there's actually a profitable opportunity that's objectively attractive to pursue in connection with expanding social benefits.

Let me build on an example from Lesson Twenty-Eight that may trigger some innovative thinking on your part: launching new enterprises. Traditionally the governments in sub-Saharan Africa have spent enormous sums received from more developed nations to train, equip, and encourage new business leaders. Most such efforts don't bear much fruit. The training and loans are received by people who want to start businesses, the funds are spent on something, the businesses eventually collapse, the loans are not repaid, and the businesspeople start looking for new loans to start another business. Those who work with such programs report that free money can be addictive, rather than helpful, for entrepreneurs.

A student of mine in Malawi, Donald Kamdonyo, Ph.D., undertook to see what could be done to help entrepreneurs in other ways. He invested a little of his own money to rent a place to hold classes about entrepreneurship for leaders of marginal small businesses. By working closely with his students, he learned that they lacked some basic disciplines needed to succeed, such as keeping personal and business funds separate, filling out the required paperwork to qualify for supplying government contracts, showing up for work on time, and paying their bills when due. He developed a course module to teach the importance of these practices and to provide practical training in how to do them properly.

Once these habits were instilled, the small businesses started to do much better. Still, many of them were operating on too little capital. Because they lacked good credit, they could not borrow to expand their businesses.

At that point, Donald began to teach lessons for applying 2,000 percent solution methods to expand sales by 20 times, reduce costs by 96 percent, and eliminate 96 percent of all investment needs. In several cases, the small businesspeople had opportunities to become government suppliers. After obtaining such contracts, they learned ways to find financing from suppliers to tide them over until such time as the government payment was made. In these activities, such entrepreneurs often began supplying goods and services that had formerly been provided by government employees. Unlike in many Western countries where government contracts are often low-margin opportunities, Donald found that the resulting profit margins were generous for low bidders. With such financing in place, these entrepreneurs were able to then bid for large private contracts and supply them, too, at high profit margins. So such private financing allowed his beneficiaries to help themselves to rapidly expand their incomes, their hiring, and their net worths.

Financing of inventory, equipment, and high-quality receivables is often done by businesses in most countries. If providing the public benefit in replacing a government activity requires having inventory and equipment, and high-quality receivables are generated, then private financing will be readily available. Most governments are on a cash basis for accounting purposes. Consequently, expanding some programs that they want to do which require more capital than the annual budget can bear may require nothing more than leasing some equipment and financing some inventory. The government receivable is generally considered to be high quality and can be turned into financing for doing such work on the government's behalf. If your beneficiaries can be hired to do some of this work while serving other beneficiaries, you'll help expand benefits even faster.

Let's now expand this example to focus, instead, on small businesses that don't have substantial government contracting opportunities, but do have substantial opportunities to replace government activities without receiving payments from the government or other organizations with good credit.

Imagine that Donald Kamdonyo, instead, offered his services to small businesspeople on a contingent-fee basis, such that they paid him a percentage of any profit increases they made above a certain level. To provide such education, Donald would need to cover his immediate income needs, plus costs for rental of any facilities, and providing any materials that he hands out, as well as any transportation and communications costs. With the spectacular improvements that some of his students experienced, the percentage of increase that he might require would not have to be very large.

From working with such students, Donald would also develop a sense of which ones have the most promising business opportunities and are best equipped to capitalize on such opportunities. If any of these organizations would not have access to government or private financing, Donald could offer to such students financing alternatives using his own resources in the forms of venture capital, mezzanine financing, convertible debt, working-capital lending, and equipment leasing. He could use the cash flow from the educational activities to establish a good credit rating that would permit him to acquire the needed capital from private sources at a reasonable cost and make such funds available selectively to his most promising students who need financing. Consequently, he might receive substantial ownership positions in some businesses that will become quite valuable after making only small initial outlays with limited risk.

Successful entrepreneurs often want to upgrade their housing. In developing nations long-term loans (mortgages) for housing are usually limited in size and duration. Consequently, there's often a shortage of quality housing. Donald could further leverage his financing activities by conservatively providing long-term lending for housing to the entrepreneurs so that their businesses would be not be harmed by such personal spending. With a large-enough equity stake taken by the entrepreneur, these loans might be actually quite low risk. If repayment records are good, Donald would eventually be able to use the mortgages as collateral to borrow at lower interest rates and increase his cash flow.

What's the key lesson? *An organization that sincerely wants to accelerate its profitable growth can be helped by increasing the current level of the social benefits by a much larger (more than 20 times) multiple than the profit increases that it gains from providing the social-benefit* *expansions in ways that replace a government activity by directly financing beneficiaries.*

Your Lesson Twenty-Nine Assignments

1. Identify places where existing government activities are being criticized, need to become more efficient, or are in short supply.

2. Consider more efficient ways to accomplish such activities.

3. Determine who will be opposed to making a change in favor of private enterprise.

4. Explore methods for providing an alternative that will not be overly threatening to those who will be opposed.

5. Develop a direct financing plan from your own organization that provides beneficiaries and taxpayers with hope.

6. Find allies who will favor such an approach and explain to them how they will benefit.

7. Develop a superior track record in providing an alternative.

8. Gradually become the dominant provider by doing a better job at lower cost while growing through just taking most of the expansion in benefit provision so others don't lose their jobs.

Lesson Thirty

Replace a Government Activity by Showing Beneficiaries How to Finance Themselves

Let the word of Christ dwell in you richly
in all wisdom, teaching and admonishing
one another in psalms and hymns and spiritual songs,
singing with grace in your hearts to the Lord.

— Colossians 3:16 (NKJV)

To me, there's no better activity than equipping people to be guided by the Bible and the Holy Spirit to advance God's Kingdom. In this lesson, we look at one possible application of such equipping: showing beneficiaries how to obtain funds for themselves and to make good use of them. As you can easily imagine, this topic was suggested to me by the centerpiece of lessons twenty-eight and twenty-nine, Dr. Donald Kamdonyo's entrepreneurship course in Malawi. Let me briefly review what I shared in those lessons.

I see such opportunities to replace government activities being good primarily in circumstances where other sources would probably not be available, while there's actually a profitable opportunity that's objectively attractive to pursue in equipping beneficiaries.

Traditionally the governments in sub-Saharan Africa have spent enormous sums that were received as foreign aid nations to train, equip, and encourage new business leaders. Most such efforts don't bear much fruit. The training and loans are received by people who want to start businesses, the funds are spent on something, the businesses eventually collapse, the loans are not repaid, and the businesspeople start looking for new loans to start another business. Those who work with such programs report that free money can be addictive, rather than helpful, for entrepreneurs.

Donald Kamdonyo, Ph.D., undertook to see what could be done to help entrepreneurs in other ways. He invested a little of his own money to rent a place to hold classes about entrepreneurship for leaders of marginal small businesses. From working closely with his students, he learned that they lacked some basic disciplines needed to succeed, such as keeping personal and business funds separate, filling out the required paperwork to qualify for supplying government contracts, showing up for work on time, and paying their bills when due. He developed a course module to teach the importance of the practices and to provide practical training in how to do them properly.

Once these habits were instilled, the small businesses started to do much better. Still, many of them were operating on too little capital. Because they lacked good credit, they could not borrow to expand their businesses.

At that point, Donald began to teach lessons for applying 2,000 percent solution methods to expand sales by 20 times, reduce costs by 96 percent, and eliminate 96 percent of all investment needs. In several cases, the small businesspeople had opportunities to become government suppliers. After obtaining such contracts, they learned ways to find financing from suppliers to tide them over until such time as the government payment was made. In these activities, such entrepreneurs often began supplying goods and services that had formerly been provided by government employees. Unlike in many

Western countries where government contracts are often low-margin opportunities, Donald found that the resulting profit margins were generous for low bidders. With such financing in place, these entrepreneurs were able to then bid for large private contracts and supply them, too, at high profit margins. So such private financing allowed his beneficiaries to help themselves to rapidly expand their incomes, their hiring, and their net worths.

Financing of inventory, equipment, and high-quality receivables is often done by businesses in most countries. If providing the public benefit in replacing a government activity requires having inventory and equipment, and high-quality receivables are generated, then private financing will be readily available. Most governments are on a cash basis for accounting purposes. Consequently, expanding some programs that they want to do which require more capital than the annual budget can bear may require nothing more than leasing some equipment and financing some inventory. The government receivable is generally considered to be high quality and can be turned into financing for doing such work on the government's behalf. If your beneficiaries can be hired to do some of this work while serving other beneficiaries, you'll help expand benefits even faster.

In Lesson Twenty-Nine, I expand this example to focus, instead, on small businesses that don't have substantial government contracting opportunities, but do have substantial opportunities to replace government activities without receiving payments from the government or other organizations with good credit.

Imagine now that Donald Kamdonyo competed, instead, for non-governmental organization (NGO) financing to provide such education and succeeded in gaining a large grant to provide training and to teach others to do the same. Consequently, his services would be provided at no charge to small businesspeople. If he received funding for at least three years, payments for such teaching could then be shifted to receiving donations from successful graduates of this educational program. Naturally, new NGO funding could also be sought.

If there were no Donald Kamdonyo in the country to do such educational work, a company could encourage its own employees to do so either as formal assignments or as volunteers to provide the seed efforts that can be expanded into the kinds of programs described here.

As a piece of this education, modules could be developed for so volunteer businesspeople could more effectively teach youngsters in primary and secondary schools. NGO funding could pay for developing and making the materials available to such volunteers.

Another approach would be to find teachers who wanted to supplement their incomes with small business activities. The teachers could be provided with free training in exchange for agreeing to do a certain amount of volunteer teaching for their students after regular teaching hours, as well as teaching local small business owners in the evenings and on weekends. The teachers would then be free to apply what they learn to their own enterprises. They could emulate the Donald Kamdonyo model I've been describing in this lesson.

Graduates of the first two courses whose businesses become more successful could be taught how to do the sort of venture-capital investing and lending described in Lesson Twenty-Nine. The result would be to add to teaching programs financing sources that would make it easier for small business owners to obtain funds or finance themselves and provide an incentive to carefully follow what the courses teach.

A particularly attractive variation on this theme would be to provide such training in ways that many of the small business owners can become providers of activities needed for your organization to begin replacing the government activity that isn't effective or efficient enough.

What's the key lesson? *An organization that sincerely wants to accelerate its profitable growth can be helped by increasing the current level of the social benefits by a much larger (more than 20 times) multiple than the profit increases that it gains from providing the social-benefit* *expansions in ways that replace a government activity by showing beneficiaries how to finance themselves.*

Your Lesson Thirty Assignments

1. Identify places where existing government activities are being criticized, need to become more efficient, or are in short supply.

2. Consider more efficient ways to accomplish such activities.

3. Determine who will be opposed to making a change in favor of private enterprise.

4. Explore methods for providing an alternative that will not be overly threatening to those who will be opposed.

5. Develop or encourage the development of an educational program to teach beneficiaries how to develop or obtain their own funds that will generate enough useful activity to provide beneficiaries and taxpayers with reasons for hope.

6. Find allies who will favor such an approach and explain to them how they will benefit.

7. Develop a superior track record in providing an alternative.

8. Gradually become the dominant provider by doing a better job at lower cost while growing through just taking most of the expansion in benefit provision so others don't lose their jobs.

Lesson Thirty-One

Replace a Private-Enterprise Activity

And may the Lord make you increase and
abound in love to one another and to all,
just as we do *to you,*
so that He may establish your hearts
blameless in holiness before
our God and Father at the coming
of our Lord Jesus Christ with all His saints.

— 1 Thessalonians 3:12-13 (NKJV)

This is a good time to remind ourselves that the main purpose of profitably expanding social benefits is to advance God's Kingdom by showing His love to those who need it most. I encourage you to memorize these verses from 1 Thessalonians 3:12-13 (NKJV) to help keep your heart and mind focused on why you are developing these solutions.

In Lesson Thirty, we concluded our examination of replacing a government activity by describing how beneficiaries could be taught to find the necessary funding for themselves. In this present lesson, we start exploring a third strategy for making the sixth complementary 2,000 percent solution: replacing a private-enterprise activity.

You might be wondering what sorts of social benefits are primarily being provided now by private enterprises. I think of banks and private enterprises that provide consumer financing as examples that have broad implications throughout society. For example, in many countries purchases of housing are mostly financed with bank credit. If that credit costs more than it should, then the availability of housing is reduced. Likewise, many people need transportation to get to work. If they cannot afford any form of motorized transit, their choices of work and their incomes can be greatly reduced. For those with little income, it may be necessary to finance even the purchase of a used motorbike for such commuting. In addition, small farmers often lack the capital needed to make profit-enhancing investments that would improve yields such as for better seeds, fertilizer, and irrigation.

You see attempts to increase such benefits through nonprofit organizations such as the Grameen Bank (supplying low-cost microlending and consumer/small business education), Habitat for Humanity (using donations and volunteers to construct low-cost homes and to finance them with no-interest loans), and technology developers that seek to deliver productivity-increasing innovations.

As you can see from these examples, changing a business model and involving a nonprofit organization can be part of such solutions. So how does such an approach relate to your organization increasing social benefits by 400 times and your organization's profits by 20 times?

Well, replacing what private enterprise provides doesn't necessarily mean that there isn't a role for enterprises that are profit-seeking to apply new business models to do so.

Here's an example from the banking world. Credit unions in the United States compete quite effectively with privately and publicly owned banks by simply having the enterprise be owned by the depositors, who are usually required to deposit a mere $5 to gain lower-cost services and lending. Such enterprises still have employees and management teams, and employ private organizations, such as accounting firms, to perform their tasks.

If a country lacked access to the kind of low-cost capital that credit unions can supply to working class and lower middle class borrowers, a private enterprise could set up such a member-owned credit union and provide the initial capital. In exchange, the private enterprise could receive a long-term contract to provide the organization with management and employees. An organization providing such services would have an economic incentive to increase social benefits as a way to grow the organization and to reduce costs so that the management contract would be more profitable. If the credit union's charter called for limits on what fees and interest rates could be charged to members, such a credit union would operate much like a traditional nonprofit credit union but with a for-profit incentive for management to expand the social benefits. Do you see how that development might occur? Naturally, there might be regulatory limitations on such a business structure that would have to be addressed or changed.

The idea of establishing new nonprofits that a for-profit organization services or benefits from isn't a new one. The American Association of Retired Persons (AARP) was originally established as a way to sell life insurance for the Colonial Penn organization. In exchange for paying to set up AARP, Colonial Penn received a long-term agreement to be the only insurance company endorsed by AARP. While that effort by Colonial Penn was transparently profit-seeking, retired persons since then have gained untold benefits from having their first government lobbying organization. Eventually, the relationship came under attack, and Colonial Penn was dropped ... in part due to not providing competitive social benefits through its endorsed insurance services. This example reminds us that we always need to be faithful in expanding God's Kingdom, rather than worshiping the money that might be added to our purses and wallets.

In other cases, a for-profit enterprise could be established to access free resources dedicated to serving social purposes, such as a private homebuilder being permitted to operate like Habitat for Humanity to build on donated land with materials provided by donors and by employing volunteer labor and then providing no interest mortgages subsidized by donated funds. Such an example is much like the credit union example I described earlier. The for-profit enterprise plays a management and operating role in what is otherwise a nonprofit activity.

Of course, there's also the potential to simply learn from and improve upon what nonprofit organizations do in cases where such organizations are the world's most effective, such as the Aravind Eye Care System. In fact, a number of for-profit imitators have been established in that industry by Aravind training and helping to improve these organizations through its fee-based consulting services. Since there are many nations where this business model for supplying vision-related benefits is not yet in place, the remaining for-profit opportunities are quite large.

Naturally, there are also situations where neither governments nor other organizations effectively provide enough social benefits. In such instances, there's an opportunity to innovate by replacing the means by which the bulk of the benefits are being provided. For engaging in this strategy, focus on those areas where private enterprise is the primary source of the offering but doesn't do so very effectively. I believe that providing vehicles and motorbikes through low-cost rentals and leases is such an opportunity.

Let me share an example. In our area, someone who has held a job for a few years can lease a new vehicle for about $200 a month. Yet someone who has been out of work for a few years would only be able to rent a used vehicle by paying cash in advance at a cost of $1,200 a month. If such a person is going to be able to keep the new job, surely there should be a way to reduce the monthly cost closer to $200 a month until such time as the person can negotiate such a deal for him- or herself. In the meantime, there's a pretty wonderful profit opportunity that will greatly expand social benefits among the newly employed.

What's the key lesson? *An organization that sincerely wants to accelerate its profitable growth can be helped by increasing the current level of the social benefits by a much larger (more than 20 times) multiple than the profit increases that it gains from providing the social-benefit expansions in ways that replace a private-enterprise activity.*

Your Lesson Thirty-One Assignments

1. Identify places where existing private-enterprise activities are being criticized, need to become more efficient, or are in short supply.

2. Consider more efficient ways to accomplish such activities.

3. Determine who will be opposed to making a change in how such benefits are provided.

4. Explore methods for providing an alternative that will not be overly threatening to those who will be opposed.

5. Find allies who will favor such an approach and explain to them how they will benefit.

6. Develop a superior track record in providing an alternative.

7. Gradually become the dominant provider by providing more value at lower cost for all stakeholders.

Lesson Thirty-Two

Replace a Private-Enterprise Activity with High Social Costs

Now Jacob cooked a stew; and
Esau came in from the field, and he was *weary.*

And Esau said to Jacob,
"Please feed me with that same red stew, *for I* am *weary."*
Therefore his name was called Edom.

But Jacob said, "Sell me your birthright as of this day."

And Esau said, "Look, I am *about to die;*
so what is *this birthright to me?"*

Then Jacob said, "Swear to me as of this day."

So he swore to him, and sold his birthright to Jacob.

And Jacob gave Esau bread and stew of lentils;
then he ate and drank, arose, and went his way.

— Genesis 25:29-34 (NKJV)

Genesis 25:29-34 (NKJV) presents a memorable example of a private transaction with high social costs. To obtain some stew, Esau sells his birthright, his most valuable possession. As the elder son, Esau was entitled to a double portion of Isaac's wealth upon his father's death. With just the two sons, Esau would have received two-thirds of the estate and Jacob but one-third. By selling his birthright, Jacob would receive two-thirds and Esau only one-third. In addition, the sale is one of a series of occasions on which Jacob took advantage of Esau, creating a rift in the family with consequences that lasted for many years. While you might think that example is extreme, some poor families in the developing world today sell their young children into indentured bondage or even slavery in exchange for the equivalent of just a few dollars.

In Lesson Thirty-One, we started exploring a third strategy: replacing a private-enterprise activity. That lesson provides several examples of how a private enterprise often indirectly increases or decreases social benefits, as well as how private organizations can work cooperatively with nonprofits to increase social benefits and profits.

In this lesson, we now turn our attention to identifying situations where private enterprises are either causing social benefits to have high costs or are doing too little to reduce such costs. In many instances, finding such circumstances will be a logical entry point for being able to consider innovations that replace existing private enterprises with improved business models.

To whet your appetite for the possibility of finding and improving upon such inefficiencies, the prior lesson cites the example of how a newly employed person might have to pay $1,200 a month in advanced cash to rent a used vehicle while someone who had been more steadily employed would pay only $200 a month for access to an identical new vehicle.

Let's begin by examining that example more closely. Why does the newly employed person need to pay so much more? The answer relates to an innovation that was designed to make offering credit much less expensive: the credit score. In the United States, individuals are assigned a credit score by evaluating their use of credit over the prior ten years: How much they borrowed, how much of any revolving lines of credit were in use, how regularly they made their payments, whether they failed to repay any borrowings, how often they applied for credit, and how much interest lenders charged. If you are steadily employed, and reasonably diligent in making your payments and not outspending your income, you'll simply keep your promises to the lenders. As a result of having done so, you will have a high credit score. People will be eager to lend to you at relatively low interest rates.

If you have been unemployed for several years, chances are that you missed some payments, defaulted on paying some of your debt, ran above your credit limits by failing to keep interest payments current, and saw interest rates on your credit cards soar through the roof. By only looking back at what has happened most recently, such a credit score will be quite low and accurately describes the credit risk of someone who doesn't have a job and needs to borrow money to buy groceries.

If the unemployed person is actually of good character, and now has a job that pays well and is likely to last for many years, the person's credit score will gradually improve and be totally repaired within ten years.

Where does the vehicle cost come in? Well, the $200 a month deal is part of a lease for 24 to 36 months after usually making a down payment of $2,000 or more. So there's a total expenditure involved of something like $6,800 to $9,200. If someone starts missing payments, there's a $2,000 cushion from the down payment to pay the lessor for the cost of repossessing the vehicle and any loss of value due to heavy usage and damage.

The newly employed person who is putting down $1,200 cash in advance monthly is renting on a daily or weekly basis. Such rates are based on the assumption of high transaction costs due to there being new paperwork daily or weekly. Also, the down payment amount is only about $300. The vehicle has an electronic tracking device on it, so it can be found and retrieved if it's not returned on time. There will probably be an economic loss of a few hundred dollars if repossession occurs that's reflected in the high daily or weekly rate.

Let's look at what could be done, instead. In the simplest example, a new business might offer multiple-month leases shorter than 24 months in length, say 6 months, with a required down payment of, say, $600 to cover almost all potential retrieval costs. If such a lessor verified and monitored employment in some way so that the lease would immediately end if the job was lost, such leasing could actually be no more risky than the cash-in-advance method when dealing with a continually employed person. If the monthly rate for such leases were set at $300 a month, that amount would build a profit cushion of $600 over six months that would more than offset any remaining potential retrieval costs. The newly employed person would be able to use the difference in cost ($300 less in just the first month and $600 subsequently each month) to catch up on old bills and possibly buy some new clothes to make a better impression at work.

As you can imagine, providing such a cost advantage means that the word would soon get around to other newly employed people who had previously been among the long-term unemployed. Consequently, the marketing cost to find such customers would probably be quite small.

Statistical studies could also help indicate other predictors of who will be a good risk for such deals. Certainly, having another organization or person provide credit (say, through providing a hold on a credit card) might be one such method. Many young people might be able to find a parent or sibling who would be willing to help in this way if unable to obtain their own credit cards.

To find such opportunities is pretty simple: Locate people who probably need more social benefits and ask them where they receive poor value from private enterprises. Candidates probably include those with low incomes, the unemployed, heads of single-parent households, large families, homeless people, and those with poor English language skills (at least in the United States). Such individuals will probably mention the need for covering emergency costs (such as to repair a vehicle needed for work or to replace a furnace in a home), as one example. Such funds are often provided now to such people at costs that exceed the equivalent of several hundred percent in annualized rates of interest, far beyond what is really needed to cover the risk of not being repaid.

What's the key lesson? *An organization that sincerely wants to accelerate its profitable growth can be helped by increasing the current level of the social benefits by a much larger (more than 20 times) multiple than the profit increases that it gains from providing the social-benefit expansions in ways that replace a private-enterprise activity with high social costs.*

Your Lesson Thirty-Two Assignments

1. Identify places where existing private-enterprise activities are being criticized, need to become more efficient, or are in short supply.

2. Consider more efficient ways to accomplish such activities.

3. Determine who will be opposed to making a change in how such benefits are provided.

4. Explore methods for providing an alternative that will not be overly threatening to those who will be opposed.

5. Find allies who will favor such an approach and explain to them how they will benefit.

6. Develop a superior track record in providing an alternative.

7. Gradually become the dominant provider by providing more value at lower cost.

Lesson Thirty-Three

Replace a Private-Enterprise Activity Providing Few Social Benefits

When He had come down from the mountain,
great multitudes followed Him.
And behold, a leper came and worshiped Him, saying,
"Lord, if You are willing, You can make me clean."

Then Jesus put out His *hand and touched him, saying,*
"I am willing; be cleansed."
Immediately his leprosy was cleansed.

And Jesus said to him,
"See that you tell no one; but go your way,
show yourself to the priest, and
offer the gift that Moses commanded,
as a testimony to them."

— Matthew 8:1-4 (NKJV)

From the time of Moses, the Israelites had great concerns about leprosy. Those who were suspected of having the disease were directed to be inspected by the priests. After having been found to have the affliction, the sufferers had to separate themselves from other Jews. Doing so meant isolation and being required to warn others to stay away by shouting, "Unclean." While there were some social benefits for those without leprosy from this practice, lepers could not go into the Temple to worship, thus harming their relationships with God. Jesus took a different approach. Rather than avoiding the touch of such a person, Jesus touched and healed him. Clearly, Jesus showed the better way to expand social benefits.

In Lesson Thirty-One, we started exploring a third strategy: replacing a private-enterprise activity. That lesson provides several examples of how private enterprises often indirectly increase or decrease social benefits, as well as how private organizations can work cooperatively with nonprofits to increase social benefits and business profits.

In Lesson Thirty-Two, we turned our attention to identifying situations where private enterprises are either causing social benefits to have high costs or are doing too little to reduce those costs. In many instances, finding such circumstances will be a logical entry point for identifying innovations to replace existing private enterprises with improved business models that will provide far more social benefits at much lower costs.

In this present lesson, we consider, instead, replacing private-enterprise activities that provide few social benefits. Cigarette manufacturing, distribution, and marketing is perhaps the best example of a fairly major industry that's usually conducted by private enterprises that produces relatively few social benefits. While medical research suggests that a high percentage of the consumption of cigarettes is related to an addiction to nicotine and other cigarette additives, many people will develop life-threatening or costly diseases from smoking cigarettes, and the quality of life will be greatly reduced for some who smoke or are exposed to such smoke. Most of the social benefits relate to the high taxes on purchasing cigarettes that are received by various governments.

Some people would look at a situation like this and decide that there's nothing inherently bad about smoking, just as long as the addiction, disease, and quality of life issues could be dealt with. Consequently, there has long been a search for a "safe" cigarette. While such research may someday produce an alternative that some people like, any increase in social benefits will come primarily from eliminating some of the social harm that smoking creates.

Another approach that some people have taken is to seek to eliminate or reduce cigarette smoking. Some businesses offer nicotine-laced gum, nicotine patches, and various cessation programs. Again, the social benefit comes from reducing social harm.

I'm unaware of any programs that primarily seek to compete with cigarette manufacturers, distributors, and marketers via adding vast quantities of social benefits. What might such an approach look like?

I cannot claim in any way to have studied this issue or to be knowledgeable about it, but some things occur to me that might work. Let me start with something I thought of while listening to a recorded book by an author who was exploring how to discipline himself to live a healthier lifestyle. He, a Jew, decided that he would strengthen his commitment by writing a check payable to the American Nazi party that would be sent if he failed in his new discipline.

Hearing that example made me wonder if some people might be motivated enough by redirecting the money normally spent on cigarettes to some socially beneficial cause to help them stop smoking cigarettes. For example, a child in slavery could be rescued for about the cost of a carton of cigarettes in the United States. I know which way I would rather spend my money. I would also feel very guilty if I knew someone was suffering in slavery because I couldn't kick my slavery to nicotine. How about you?

A private company could found a service designed to help a smoker identify some socially beneficial uses for the money and time involved that would cause a dramatic and lasting change in the smoker's behavior. Such a service would not only help reduce social harm, but the service would also lead to creating large amounts of social benefits. Does that example make sense to you?

One of the things I like about this thought process for designing new business activities is that it helps to identify bigger and more significant business-model innovations than what traditional business thinking has attempted or accomplished.

This thought process also makes it easy to identify targets of opportunity: Look for large combinations of social harm being created that are offset by virtually no social benefits. In the process you are sure to be able to innovate with something that will replace a good portion of what the traditional industry is doing. Does that make sense to you?

What's the key lesson? *An organization that sincerely wants to accelerate its profitable growth can be helped by increasing the current level of the social benefits by a much larger (more than 20 times) multiple than the 20-times profit increases that it gains from providing the social-benefit expansions in ways that replace a private-enterprise activity that provides few social benefits.*

Your Lesson Thirty-Three Assignments

1. Identify places where existing private-enterprise activities are being criticized because of their social harm or limited provision of social benefits.

2. Consider ways to eliminate the social harm and create vast amounts of social benefits that will be appealing to those who purchase or employ the current offerings.

3. Determine who will be opposed to making such a change.

4. Explore methods for providing an alternative that will not be overly threatening to those who will be opposed.

5. Find allies who will favor such an approach and explain to them how they will benefit.

6. Develop a superior track record in providing an alternative.

7. Gradually become the dominant provider by reducing social harm while greatly increasing social benefits that are considered highly desirable.

Lesson Thirty-Four

Replace a Private-Enterprise Activity by Greatly Increasing Social Benefits

So when they had eaten breakfast,
Jesus said to Simon Peter,
"Simon, son *of Jonah,*
do you love Me more than these?"

He said to Him,
"Yes, Lord; You know that I love You."

He said to him, "Feed My lambs."

He said to him again a second time,
"Simon, son *of Jonah, do you love Me?"*

He said to Him,
"Yes, Lord; You know that I love You."

He said to him, "Tend My sheep."

He said to him the third time,
"Simon, son *of Jonah, do you love Me?"*

Peter was grieved because
He said to him the third time,
"Do you love Me?"
And he said to Him,
"Lord, You know all things;
You know that I love You."

Jesus said to him, "Feed My sheep."

"Most assuredly, I say to you,
when you were younger, you girded yourself
and walked where you wished;
but when you are old,
you will stretch out your hands, and
another will gird you and
carry you *where you do not wish."*

This He spoke, signifying by what death
he would glorify God.
And when He had spoken this,
He said to him, "Follow Me."

— John 21:15-19 (NKJV)

In Matthew 4 (NKJV), four fishermen leave their family business to become disciples of Jesus. Over the next three years, Jesus trained them to become fishers of men, people who could help unbelievers find their way to Salvation through faith in Jesus. During that time, Peter is described in the Gospel accounts as being the disciple most able to discern that Jesus is the Messiah. However, Peter could also be hot headed and blurt out inappropriate comments. Before Jesus was arrested, Peter told Jesus that he would gladly die to protect

Him. In response, Jesus prophesied that before the cock crowed three times, Peter would deny Him on three occasions. Such denials happened the following morning while Jesus was being interrogated. Peter was mortified when he realized what he had done. In these verses from John 21, we see the resurrected Savior redeeming Peter's three denials by allowing him to affirm his love for Jesus three times. With the arrival of the Holy Spirit on Pentecost, as described in Acts 2 (NKJV), the transformation of Peter was complete and his sermon to the multitude that day led to 3,000 people being saved, the beginning of the Christian church as we know it today. Has any transformation of someone from producing one kind of Godly benefit (catching fish to feed people) into a new kind (leading the church and helping many gain Salvation) ever been as fruitful for God's Kingdom as this one?

In Lesson Thirty-One, we began exploring a third strategy: Replace a private-enterprise activity. That lesson provides several examples of how private enterprises often indirectly increase or decrease social benefits, as well as how private organizations can work cooperatively with nonprofits to increase social benefits and profits. In Lesson Thirty-Two, we turned our attention to identifying situations where private enterprises are either providing social benefits with high costs or are doing little to reduce benefit costs. In many instances, finding such circumstances will be a logical entry point for considering innovations to replace private-enterprise activities with improved business models that provide far more social benefits at much lower costs, while also serving as a more effective source of the primary offerings such enterprises make available. In Lesson Thirty-Three, we also considered replacing private-enterprise activities that provide few social benefits.

In this present lesson, we now take a different approach: searching for private-enterprise activities for which social benefits can be greatly increased without regard to how substantial or small, costly, or inexpensive these social benefits currently are.

Let me start by sharing an example of what I mean. Think of for-profit universities. Some of these learning institutions are excellent while others could make considerable improvements. When someone attends such an institution (in person or online), there's potential for increasing social benefits. A student might add or improve a skill that enables her or him to accomplish more in activities with important social consequences. For instance, a business student might develop skill in providing new offerings that generate social benefits in an industry where they have not been previously available. If that business becomes a model for others, emulation could spread the social benefits quite a bit farther.

Such opportunities potentially have a large multiplier effect. In making that comment, I'm reminded by how much a checking-account deposit increases the capital base of a bank. For instance, if the government requirement is that 10 percent of deposits be retained in cash or government securities, a dollar deposited in a bank can be lent out as nine dollars, thus expanding the bank's capital base by a factor of nine.

I believe that the multiplier for expanding social benefits can often be quite a bit larger. That's because there's a physical multiplier (much like the bank deposit has a financial multiplication effect) as well as a multiplier related to emulation by other organizations. So expanding social benefits is more like the difference between increasing by eight thousand times than by nine times. Let me explain how. The direct effect from the business itself is probably more than a twenty-fold increase in benefits. Then, the multiplication through customers and other beneficiaries being able to use the increased benefits expands the benefit total by more than four hundred times. Adding the copycat factor from other organizations adds another twenty-fold or more increase to the four hundred times increase. Do you see that?

Let me be more specific. I once worked with a student who intended to enroll in a business school. In the course of assisting her, I noticed that one university she applied to required creating social benefits as part of its entrepreneurship program. As a result, those who study in this program will all be seeking to add social benefits to any new enterprises they develop. Let's consider what the potential effects might be.

Instead of the multiplier of affecting one student somewhat randomly, in this case the business school is affecting hundreds of students who intend to become founders and CEOs of innovative organizations. Such students may establish new business models, industries, and types of social benefits. By formally learning how to add social benefits, the students will be much more likely to apply their skills in this way. If the social-benefit innovations are combined with many other innovations (as the innovations would be for those who belong to The Billionaire Entrepreneurs' Master Mind or who have been reading and applying *Business Basics*, *Advanced Business*, *Advanced Business for Innovation*, and *Advanced Business for Social Benefits*), there's also a major multiplication potential added.

Let me bring this observation about multiplying benefits a little closer to home. Look at your business. Is there some way that your customers, end users, suppliers, partners, investors, lenders, distributors, employees, employees' families, community, and the general public could provide vastly more social benefits in some way that would also improve your business volume and profits? If so, then consider adding ways that your organization and some or all of these stakeholder groups could also find it advantageous to educate still more people to do the same or related social-benefit-enhancing activities. If you do that, you'll find that your organization will be expanding social benefits to an exponential degree not too dissimilar from what the business school is doing that I described earlier.

I look forward to hearing your thoughts about how you might apply this lesson.

What's the key lesson? *An organization that sincerely wants to accelerate its profitable growth can be helped by increasing the current level of the social benefits by a much larger (more than 20 times) multiple* *than the profit increases that it gains from providing the social-benefit expansions in ways that replace a private-enterprise activity for which social benefits can be greatly increased.*

Your Lesson Thirty-Four Assignments

1. Identify places where existing private-enterprise activities are producing less than 1 percent of the potential social benefits.

2. Consider ways to create vast amounts of social benefits that will be appealing to those who purchase or employ the current offerings.

3. Determine who will be opposed to making such a change.

4. Explore methods for providing an alternative that will not be overly threatening to those who will be opposed.

5. Find allies who will favor such an approach and explain to them how they will benefit.

6. Develop a superior track record in providing an alternative.

7. Gradually become the dominant provider by greatly increasing social benefits that are considered highly desirable.

Afterword

I have been crucified with Christ;
it is no longer I who live,
but Christ lives in me; and
the life *which I now live in the flesh*
I live by faith in the Son of God,
who loved me and gave Himself for me.

— Galatians 2:20 (NKJV)

If you have been faithful in reading and applying *Business Basics*, *Advanced Business*, *Advanced Business for Innovation*, and *Advanced Business for Social Benefits* (and hopefully *Excellent Solutions* and *Excellent Leadership*, as well), you've been on a transformative journey that has made you more like Christ, the important sanctification that follows accepting Salvation. You have prayed for being, and have been, filled and refilled with the Holy Spirit on many occasions. As a result of listening to the Holy Spirit, you now have a better idea of what your calling is for advancing God's Kingdom. Since you have been drawn to one or more of these books, undoubtedly your purpose is aligned with at least some aspects of their lessons. Take that purpose and calling seriously. Pray for added guidance to keep a light drawing you to where you should be going. God has a great plan for your life! I can hardly wait to see the results of that plan. If I can be of any assistance to you during your discipleship journey, please contact me at save_more_souls@yahoo.com/. May God bless you, your family, and all you do in the name of Jesus!

Appendix One

Donald Mitchell's Testimony

He will lift you up.

Humble yourselves
in the sight of the Lord,
and He will lift you up.

— James 4:10 (NKJV)

Let me share with you how I became a Christian so you'll know where I'm coming from with regard to encouraging you to become a Christian and to be fruitful in Godly contributions for creating and implementing breakthrough solutions.

There has been a long commitment to the Lord in our family. For example, I remember my great-grandmother, Edith Foster, reading the Bible every day. As a youngster, my mother regularly took me to Sunday school. It was my least favorite activity; sleeping was much preferred. I did enjoy listening to sermons, but it was frowned on to take youngsters to the adult services where the sermons were given.

If I pretended to be asleep, mom would sometimes let me stay home on Sundays. I was pretty good at pretending, and I soon was the biggest backslider in my Sunday school grade. Fortunately, it was an evangelical church so my classmates were always cooking up schemes to get me to attend again. Because of my high opinion of myself, I would always return if invited to play my clarinet for the congregation.

By the time I turned thirteen, I was pretty full of myself. There wasn't much room for God in there alongside my exaggerated opinion of myself.

One day at home while my family was away for a drive, I felt really sick. By the time they returned, I was delirious. Within an hour, I was in the hospital where I would stay for two weeks as I barely survived a bad case of double pneumonia.

My physician, Dr. Helmsley, was an observant Christian and worried about my soul because my life was in jeopardy. He talked to me about our Heavenly Father, Jesus, and the Holy Spirit twice a day when he stopped by to check on me. These conversations were when I first learned how to become a Christian through being born again. I also came to realize that I couldn't stop sinning on my own. I needed a Savior, Jesus Christ! After I recovered, he took my mom and me to a tent revival meeting.

Having recovered from the illness, I soon pushed God out of my life again. During the next year, I was, instead, very caught up in athletics. When I was in ninth grade, I desperately wanted to make a contribution to our junior high track team, which had a remote chance of winning the big meet. Our coach, Mr. Layman, told each of us exactly what had to be accomplished for the team to win. I was determined to do my part. I had to come in first!

But that wasn't likely to happen. Based on past performances, there were at least two people who could out leap me in the standing broad jump, my main event. To make such a jump, you stand on a slightly raised, forward-tilted board and spring outward as far as you can into a sand-filled pit. After two of the three jumping rounds, I knew it was hopeless. I was in sixth place and four of the competitors' jumps were longer than I had ever gone before. I also didn't like the board we were using.

Remembering that we should call on God when we need help, I thought of praying ... but what I wanted was so trivial in God's terms that I didn't think it was worthy of prayer. So I decided to make God an offer instead: "Dear God, help me win this event, and I'm yours forever." After all, if He came through, any doubts I had about God would be dispelled.

I stepped onto the broad-jump board and felt very calm. I did my routine and took off into the air. Instantly, I felt light as a feather cradled in a large, gentle hand that was lifting me. I was dropped softly at the far end of the pit. I had outleapt everyone and gone more than six inches past my best previous jump. I couldn't believe it. Then I remembered my promise to God, thanked Him, repented my sins, accepted Jesus as my Lord and Savior, and ran off to tell everyone on the team.

Even more remarkable, I was the only person on the team who performed up to the plan. Knowing what had to be done had probably given us performance anxiety, and people underperformed because they didn't believe they could do what the team needed. I also suspect that God wanted to make a point with me that I needed Him.

After a few days, I started to think that perhaps I'd just developed a new broad-jump technique and God didn't have a role at all. God soon dispelled that thought by making sure that my jumps for the rest of my life were much shorter than I had jumped when He lifted me up.

Since then, God has been speaking to me on a regular basis through the Holy Spirit. I have learned to pay attention and act promptly. When I pursue my own ideas, things don't go so well. When I follow His directions, things work out great. That's my secret to high performance, and I just wanted to share it with you so you could benefit, too. He knows the answers, even when you and I don't ... which is most of the time.

As a management consultant, the Holy Spirit has often filled me with knowledge about what the consequences of one set of actions would be compared to another for my clients. Naturally, I always recommended as the Holy Spirit directed me. Clients often told me that they were impressed by how certain I was of my conclusions and of how persuasive I could be in describing the advantages of whatever recommendations were made. Once again, the explanatory words came from the Holy Spirit, rather than from me.

Unfortunately, I wasn't comfortable in my younger days sharing my faith with clients, and I wrongly gave many people the impression that I was the author of the solutions rather than merely the transmitter. I wish I had been more faithful in this regard. I apologize to my clients for having missed so many great witnessing opportunities with them.

I didn't always listen as well as I should in making decisions that primarily affected me, but God would always do something to get my attention. Here's an example. I made an investment that I hoped would reduce my taxes in addition to making some money. I didn't have a good feeling from the Holy Spirit at the time, and I shouldn't have invested.

My tax return was later audited by the Internal Revenue Service concerning that investment. It turned out I was in the wrong for the deductions I had taken. Anticipating a big tax bill plus penalties and interest, you can imagine my astonishment when the revised tax return showed me owing no additional money to the government even though I had lost on the audit issues. I knew that result was a gift from God, and I was overwhelmed by His wisdom and power in protecting me. Praise God for His mercy!

I rededicated my life to Jesus in 1995, and I have enjoyed great peace since then. I have also done a lot better in being obedient to the Holy Spirit and to what the Bible tells us to do in all aspects of my life. Many blessings have been mine since then.

After being told by God to start The 400 Year Project (demonstrating how everyone in the world could make improvements twenty times faster and more effectively than normal with no additional resources) in 1995, I continued to receive His instructions. In

2005, for example, God told me to start explaining to people how to live their lives by gaining more joy from what they already have.

In the summer of 2006, I began to see how The 400 Year Project could be brought to a successful conclusion (as I reported in *Adventures of an Optimist*, Mitchell and Company Press, 2007). Realizing that perhaps I had devoted too much of my attention to this one challenge, I began to seek ways to rebalance my life. One of those rebalancing methods was to spend more time communing with God through prayer, Scriptural studies, attending church services and Bible classes, and listening more to the still, small voice within.

For several years I had been enjoying the devotionals sent to me daily over the Internet by evangelist Bill Keller. One of those devotionals speared me like an arrow that summer. The evangelist reminded his readers that our responsibility as believers is to share our faith with others through our example and sharing the Gospel message from the Bible. Not feeling well equipped to do more than try to be a good example, I began to pray about what else I should be doing.

The next day, my answer came: I was to launch a global contest to locate the most effective ways that souls were being saved and be sure that information was shared widely. This knowledge would be a blessing for those who wished to fulfill the Great Commission to spread the Good News of Jesus as commanded in Matthew 28:18-20 (NKJV):

> And Jesus came and spoke to them, saying, "All authority has been given to Me in heaven and on earth. Go therefore and make disciples of all the nations, baptizing them in the name of the Father and of the Son and of the Holy Spirit, teaching them to observe all things that I have commanded you; and lo, I am with you always, *even* to the end of the age."

The contest winners were Jubilee Worship Center in Hobart, Indiana, and Step by Step Ministries in Porter, Indiana. You can read their stories and learn amazingly effective ways to help unsaved people choose to accept Salvation in *Witnessing Made Easy: Yes, You Can Make a Difference* (Jubilee Worship Center Step by Step Press, 2010) by Bishop Dale P. Combs, Lisa Combs, Jim Barbarossa, Carla Barbarossa, and me. Six of the many other worthy ideas and practices from the contest for leading more people to learn about and some to be moved by the Holy Spirit to pledge their lives to Jesus are described in a second book, *Ways You Can Witness: How the Lost Are Found* (Salvation Press, 2010) by Cherie Hill, Roger de Brabant, Drew Dickens, Gael Torcise, Wendy Lobos, Herpha Jane Obod, Gisele Umugiraneza, and me.

Let me tell you another interesting thing about my life with Jesus. When my daughter was about a year old, I suffered what resembled a stroke that caused me to start to become paralyzed. As I could feel my face's muscles freezing, I immediately prayed to Jesus to stop the paralysis and He did. I was left with a lot of pain and numbness on the left side of my body and was very weak for over a year.

Part of that pain continued for the next twenty-two years until, on November 8, 2009, I asked two of my pastors during a communion service to pray in the name of Jesus that the remaining pain be removed. During the prayer, the pain started leaving immediately and was totally gone within a half hour. As I felt the pain leaving me, through some power traveling inch by inch down my body, I was overcome with gratitude and fell on my knees in thanks.

That wasn't the only time He recently healed me. Encouraged by that miraculous experience, I came forward again on December 19, 2010, during another communion service to request prayer for relief from the pain in my wrists that was making it difficult for me to write books to serve Him and to do my other work. Knowing that my mother had been plagued with arthritis, I assumed it was a similar onset for me. My pastors were occupied with prayers for other members of the congregation. This time an elder of the church and his wife anointed me with oil and prayed for me. Almost immediately, my whole body shook violently in a way that I couldn't stop. Gradually, the shaking was reduced until it stopped after about half an hour, and my wrist pain was totally gone. It has not returned. I was even more overwhelmed that He had healed me again. Can anyone appreciate all the goodness that God has in store for us?

Let me share yet another miraculous healing (not the last that I've experienced). I've always been troubled with many respiratory and food allergies and sensitivities. In my sixties, these problems had grown worse. I finally reached the point where it was difficult to be in the same room with other people, due to my reactions to any deodorants and scents they were using. During still another communion service on January 16, 2012, two pastors again prayed for me to be relieved of these problems so that I could be a better witness for Him. Once again, power filled my body. My allergies and sensitivities were gone in a few minutes. Since then, they haven't returned. It has made a huge improvement in my life and in my ability to be a witness for Christ.

I have also been saved by God from what I believed to be certain death on twelve occasions, most recently on July 2, 2013. I won't go into all of these events, but I did want you to be aware that He is always touching all aspects of my life in beneficial ways.

While it's up to God to decide if and when He wants to heal us or to protect us from harm, it's certainly reassuring to know that He has the ability and power to do anything He wants.

Glory be to God! Praise Him always! His miracles, grace, and mercy never end. I am so happy and honored to be His servant and witness to you.

Appendix Two

Brief Profiles of Organizations from Their Web Sites

But to him who does not work but believes on Him
who justifies the ungodly, his faith is accounted for righteousness,
just as David also describes the blessedness of the man
to whom God imputes righteousness apart from works:

"Blessed are those whose lawless deeds are forgiven,
And whose sins are covered;
Blessed is the man to whom
the LORD shall not impute sin."

— Romans 4:5-8 (NKJV)

Grameen Bank Web Site

Date: May 15, 2011

Beloved owners and honoured members of Grameen Bank:

Thirty-five years ago, I did not know that I would start a bank, and that I would lend to poor people, especially to poor rural women. Like many other teachers, I was busy teaching in the classroom, far from the realities on the ground. But Jobra village took my future into a completely different direction. I saw, first hand, how the loan sharks enslaved the villagers; I thought that if I were to lend money to the poor, then the villagers could be free from the grasp of the loan sharks. That is what I did. I never imagined that this would become my calling in life. I learned a lot sitting and talking with the women of Jobra; I came to know about things which I had never imagined. I longed to do whatever I could to help them. With my students, I was able to help the women in a small way. Acting as the guarantor, I was able to arrange loans from the bank for the poor people of the village. Alongside the loans, I added a savings program. At that time, women in the village did not have the capacity to save. The savings program started with 25 paisa in savings per week. Today the total amount of savings by the borrowers stands at 6 billion Taka!

Our members, when we started, did not know how to read or write. We started to teach them to write their name, with sticks in the dirt.

We organized workshops. At these workshops, you told me stories about your lives. ... From these, the "Sixteen Decisions" came into being. Those "Sixteen Decisions" have become a part of Grameen Bank. "At our son's wedding we will not take dowry; we will not take dowry. At our daughter's wedding we will not pay dowry; we will not pay dowry." "We will educate our children, at least up to class sixteen." "We shall grow vegetables all the year round. We shall eat plenty of them and sell the surplus." "Discipline, Unity, Courage and Hard work – in all walks of our lives," "We shall drink water from the tube well; if it is not available, we shall boil water and drink it." These are just some of the decisions. ....

You became united with each other. You vowed with deep resolve that you would bring prosperity to your families. That is why from the "Grameen Bank Project," you managed to create "Grameen Bank." And you became the owners of this bank. Gradually, you were able to realize each of the Sixteen Decisions. You increased the amount of savings that you hold, many times over. You have educated your children. Through Educational Loans, many of them are today studying to be doctors and engineers. Many of your children have completed their education and are now doctors, engineers and professors. ....

May the blessings of God be with you.

Yours faithfully,
Professor Muhammad Yunus

Aravind Eye Care System Web Site

Started in 1976 as an 11 bed hospital in Madurai, Aravind now has branches at Theni, Tirunelveli, Coimbatore, Pondicherry, Dindigul and Tirupur. The hospitals provide high quality and affordable services to the rich and poor alike, yet are financially self-supporting. They have well-equipped speciality clinics with comprehensive support facilities.

In the year ending March 2013, 3.1 million outpatients were treated and over 370,000 surgeries were performed.

To reach out to the rural Tamil Nadu, Aravind has established its primary eye care facility named, vision centres. The community eye clinics take care of the ophthalmic needs of a semi urban population.

Aravind Eye Care System is a collaborating centre for the World Health Organization with a mandate to design and offer training programmes to eye care personnel at different professional levels, from around the world, in the development and implementation of efficient and sustainable eye care programmes. Aravind's training programmes cater to all levels of ophthalmic personnel — these are intended not only for ophthalmologists but also for ophthalmic technicians, opticians, clinical assistants, outreach coordinators and health care managers. Aravind offers several structured training programmes.

Grameen Danone Foods Ltd.

30% of all Bangladeshis and 56% of Bangladeshi children under the age of 5 suffer from moderate to severe malnutrition. In general the country has some of the highest child and maternal malnutrition rates according to the UNICEF State of the World's Children Report 2008. This in itself is a human tragedy. Malnutrition, however, is also a major impediment to development: malnourished people become sick more easily, can work less and find it more difficult to study. While Bangladesh produces sufficient rice to nourish its people, diets often lack vital nutrients such as vitamins and minerals.

Grameen Danone Foods was founded in 2006 in order to fight malnutrition. The joint venture produces a yoghurt enriched with crucial nutrients at a price of 6 BDT (= 0.06 EUR) which even the poorest can afford. However, Grameen Danone Foods affects people's lives not only by improving their health. Benefits exist along the whole value chain. The milk for the yoghurt is purchased from microfarmers. The production is designed in such a way as to give as many people as possible a job. Sales ladies distribute the yoghurt door-to-door and receive a 10% provision. Unsold yoghurts are taken back. In total, Grameen Danone Foods is responsible for the creation of about 1,600 jobs within a 30 km radius around the plant. There is also an environmental aspect: Solar energy is used for heating up the water which is used for cleaning the installation and preheating water for the main boilers. In addition the packaging of the yoghurt is fully biodegradable.

Grameen Danone plans to expand. Within the next 10 years, more plants will be established and several hundred distribution jobs will be created. The Danone Communities Fund has been created to support this endeavor. At the beginning of 2007, the independent NGO, The Global Alliance for Improved Nutrition, launched a trial designed to test the benefits from regular consumption of the yoghurt. In November 2011, the preliminary study results were released saying that the impact of the Grameen Danone yoghurt shows a positive impact on growth and cognitive performance of children.

Newman's Own Web Site

In 1982, Newman's Own started as a tiny boutique operation – parchment labels on elegant wine bottles that Paul Newman filled with his homemade salad dressing and gave to his neighbors as holiday gifts. He expected train wrecks along the way and, instead, got one astonishment followed by another.

But in these thirty years we have earned over $400 million, all of which we've given to countless charities. How to account for this massive success? We haven't the slightest idea but one thing we do know is we're not stopping.

Today, Newman's Own produces nearly 100 individual food products across 9 categories. Always great tasting, always top quality, just the way our founder, Paul Newman, insisted. We'll always follow his vision for putting quality first. The result: You end up with a pretty darn good meal.

Paul's craft was acting, his passion was auto racing, his love was his family and friends. But his heart and soul were dedicated to helping make the world a better place. His commitment to philanthropy was clear – he used his influence, gave of his financial resources, and personally volunteered to advance humanitarian and social causes around the world. While Paul Newman was a Hollywood star of extraordinary celebrity and a person recognized for exceptional commitment and leadership for philanthropy, he lived his life as an ordinary person, which he always considered himself. He was a man of abundant good humor, generosity, and humility.

RECYCLA Chile, S.A. Web Site

At RECYCLA we aim to contribute to Corporate Social Responsibility (CSR), principally through the recycling of electronic, electrical and non-ferrous metal wastes by applying green production technology and generating worker re-training programs. Also, we offer consulting services to companies and organizations, drawing on our wide range of experience with sustainability issues to help them incorporate more sustainable practices into their production and brand.

At RECYCLA the focus of our company is innovation and sustainability for the benefit of society. We are a "social business venture" that seeks innovative and financially sustainable solutions to social problems.

We know that technology users in Chile and in the rest of the world are beginning to recognize electronic waste as a significant environmental issue. However, there is still a long way to go. For this reason, at RECYCLA we are committed to getting businesses and communities involved with concrete efforts to recycle.

Our company incorporates people with criminal records and women living in halfway houses in the recycling process as a way to provide them with a work opportunity that will help them achieve job stability and decrease the rate of recidivism.

Here at RECYCLA, through our Triple Bottom Line model, we aim to contribute to sustainable social development by synergizing economic growth with environmental preservation and social justice.

www.ingramcontent.com/pod-product-compliance
Lightning Source LLC
Chambersburg PA
CBHW072259210326
41519CB00057B/1879
9780692453933